The Imagineering Way

By The Imagineers

EDITIONS

New York

The Imagineering Way

The following are registered trademarks of The Walt Disney Company: Audio-Animatronics®, Dinoland, U.S.A., *Disneyland*® Resort, *Disneyland*® Paris, Disney's *California Adventure*™ Park, Epcot®, Imagineering, Imagineers, It's Tough to Be a Bug®, New Orleans Square, Space Mountain, Splash Mountain, *Walt Disney World*® Resort.

"The Twilight Zone®" is a registered trademark of CBS, Inc., and is used pursuant to a license from CBS, Inc.

"One Little Spark" Words and Music by Richard M. Sherman and Robert B. Sherman. ©1982 Wonderland Music Company, Inc. All Rights Reserved. Reprinted by permission.

A Camphor Tree Book
Design and layout by Bruce Gordon
Sketches of "Figment" created by Larry Nikolai

Disney Editions
Wendy Lefkon
Editorial Director

Jody Revenson
Editor

For information address:
Disney Editions
114 Fifth Avenue
New York, New York 10011-5690

Printed in the United States of America

First Edition
10 9 8 7 6 5 4 3 2

Library of Congress Cataloging-in-Publication Data on file.
ISBN 0-7868-5401-4

Visit www.disneyeditions.com

Take a Chance

> ## "In the lexicon of youth …
> ## there is no such word as 'fail'!"
> —*Edward Bulwer–Lytton*

I wonder how many times these sturdy old words have been used in graduation speeches each year. They take me back to my own high-school days, when I had my first pair of white flannel trousers and the world ahead held no heartbreak or fear.

Certainly, we have all had this confidence at one time in our lives, though most of us lose it as we grow older. Perhaps, because of my work, I've been lucky enough to retain a shred of this youthful quality. But sometimes, as I look back on how tough things were, I wonder if I'd go through it again. I hope I would.

When I was about twenty-one, I went broke for the first time. I slept on chair cushions in my "studio" in Kansas City and ate cold beans out of a can. But I took another look at my dream and set out for Hollywood.

Foolish? Not to a youngster. An older person might have had too much "common sense" to do it. Sometimes I wonder if "common sense" isn't another way of saying "fear." And "fear" too often spells failure.

In the lexicon of youth there is no such word as "fail." Remember the story about the boy who wanted to march in the circus parade? When the show came to town, the bandmaster needed a trombonist, so the boy signed up. He hadn't marched a block before the fearful noises from his horn caused two old ladies to faint and a horse to run away. The bandmaster demanded, "Why didn't you tell me you couldn't play the trombone?" And the boy said, "How did I know? I never tried before!"

Many years ago, I might have done just what that boy did. Now I'm a grandfather and have a good many gray hairs and what a lot of people call common sense. But if I'm no longer young in age, I hope I stay young enough in spirit never to fear failure—young enough still to take a chance and march in the parade.

Walt Disney
Animator, Dreamer, Father

Riding with Imagineers

When I first started at Disney publishing in 1994, I embarked on a project with a team at Walt Disney Imagineering to create a book that would tell the history of the Imagineers and offer some insight into this most interesting and mysterious of Disney divisions. That roller-coaster ride of an experience resulted in the very successful publication of *Walt Disney Imagineering— A Behind the Dreams Look at Making the Magic Real*. (In fact, that book is still in print and selling today.)

But once you take a ride with the Imagineers, something happens to you. And I couldn't help but think there was another book about Imagineering that needed to be written to offer readers a taste of the experience I had enjoyed working with this creative group.

After many meetings and conversations in our offices at Disney Publishing, I approached the Imagineering team once again and suggested that they somehow put down on paper the essence of what the Imagineering culture and environment means, and how that very culture allows them to create their magic.

And to heighten the challenge, I asked them to always keep in mind that the goal was to offer readers wonderful essays and anecdotes they would be able to absorb and somehow adapt to help them live more creative lives.

The Imagineering Way is the result of our next experiment. I encourage you to read it in its entirety because each and every page has something to offer, regardless of your age, your occupation, or your outlook on life. But read it in any order that suits you since we've organized it without any particular organizing principles—perhaps the first hint of how an Imagineer approaches life.

One more tip: as you read these entertaining anecdotes and insightful stories, find yourself on these pages and apply the ideas put forth to your own life, be it at home, work, or simply driving along the road.

Wendy Lefkon

Editorial Director, Disney Editions (and Honorary Imagineer)

The Formula Is There Is No Formula

When it comes to creativity, anything goes. Creativity, in its purest essence, means the mind is free to imagine any possibility. The sky's the limit. In its purest sense, there are no rules! Therefore, when our Imagineering "book team"—charged by the publisher with producing a book about "how to control and harness the power of creativity the Imagineering way"—first met for the purpose of formulating a structure for this book, we immediately recognized the dilemma. The very idea of establishing a structure for a book about creativity is contrary to creativity itself. The formula for creativity is that there is no formula!

Although Imagineers follow no established formula when it comes to "making the magic," we do define our goals and establish clear objectives prior to embarking on any project. And since each and every creative endeavor we take on is unique, our goals and objectives usually vary from project to project and challenge to challenge. Every new project comes with an obstacle course of unknowns that forces us to think and imagine in new and different, and sometimes even impossible ways. Perhaps that force, in itself, is the power of creativity. And if there is a trick to harnessing that power of creativity, it is not to try to control the imagination, but rather to set it free!

When Imagineers are plugged into the power of unbridled creativity, our free-soaring imaginations always seem to carry us toward discovery and subsequent practical (and sometimes impractical, as the case may be) application. Fueled by a mixture of passion and curiosity, we're not afraid to dive into the unknown and try something new and different because we faithfully follow the philosophies of our founder, Walt Disney, who said that "fear" too often spells failure.

Many people never allow their creative abilities to surface because they fear what might happen. They fear failure. They fear feeling silly or inferior. They fear what others might think. They fear, worst of all, that they are not creative! Ultimately, they succumb to this fear and do nothing. Nothing is worse than doing nothing!

Fear, then, is the worst enemy of creativity. That is why whenever we have a "blue sky" brainstorming session at Imagineering, we go into it with the understanding there is no such thing as a bad idea. No matter how silly or dumb an idea may sound, we let all those "what ifs" out. We toss fear right out the door and open wide the window of opportunity for the best view of every possibility. We never shield our eyes from the brilliance of a creative spark because we believe that when you see through the eyes of imagination, anything can happen. You never know what you're capable of doing until you start dreaming and doing it. Take the chance.

Anyone can imagine and anyone can dream. But it's the "do" part that scares away most dreamers. And that is what we decided this book should really be about: if you can dream it, you can do it!

Who better to expound on this Imagineering philosophy (and motto) than the "dream and do crew"—the Imagineers themselves? Our book team decided the best way to "unstructure" this book was to take a chance and ask our fellow Imagineers to submit a series of essays—and not necessarily written—about their own experiences with, and philosophies about, harnessing the power of creativity. How did setting their imagination free help them to solve a creative problem? How did this experience help them not only to dream but ultimately to do? Truly, we could imagine no better peek inside the Imagineering creative process than one collectively provided by those who are totally immersed in it every day. Whether an engineer, architect, artist, writer, project manager, special effects technician, landscape designer—whatever—each Imagineer is a storyteller. So we asked them to share their own stories about marching in the Imagineering parade. As you read them, remember that when it comes to creativity, Imagineers will tell you that anything goes. So toss your fears out the window, and here goes!

The Imagineers

To illustrate our book, I thought it would be fun to create some sketches of Figment (the mischievous dragon host of Journey Into Imagination at Epcot). Out of all the Disney characters, I believe he is the closest embodiment of what we do and stand for.

Larry Nikolai
Senior Conceptual Designer, Creative Development

So Who Do We Think We Are, Writing a Book Like This?

The First Question:

What, exactly, is Imagineering?

Well, mostly, it's a state of mind. It's a freedom to dream, to create, and mostly, to do.

The word "Imagineering" is a marriage of the words "imagination" and "engineering." We not only dream big but we build those dreams as well.

We really *do* make dreams come true.

In December 1952, Walt Disney gathered a handpicked handful of his most highly respected artists, animators, and designers. He dubbed his crew "Imagineers," and led them on a mission to reinvent the traditional amusement park, fulfilling a vision for a clean, friendly place where families —adults and children—could have fun together. A place that would be called "Disneyland."

In the half century that followed, literally thousands of incredibly talented individuals from more than a hundred disciplines have proudly worn the title "Imagineer."

Our mission is (and always has been) to grow and expand Walt's vision, to keep it moving forward through all the technological and cultural changes our world is undergoing, without losing sight of the core concept of family-friendly fun.

And we've been pretty successful.

At Walt Disney Imagineering, the current incarnation of Walt's original team of Imagineers, we've designed and built every attraction at every Disney resort around the world. Our parks and attractions have entertained hundreds of millions of guests in California, Florida, France, and Japan. All across the globe, the sun never sets on a Disney park.

The Second Question:

Just how did we get to be so wise, anyway?

Well, over the years, we've found ourselves face-to-face with some pretty gnarly challenges—everything from dealing with major governments to dealing with each other. We've faced technical challenges, emotional challenges, budget and schedule challenges, and, most of all, the overwhelming reality of keeping a dream alive in a world of concrete and steel, exit signs, politics, gravity, and physics.

Sometimes we've succeeded, and sometimes we've failed. Collectively and individually, we've learned a lot over the past fifty years.

Do we really have the answers? Of course not. But by retelling the stories gathered here, perhaps each of us will make a discovery or two that will keep us moving forward when we come face-to-face with the next big challenge.

Moving forward, after all, is the most important thing there is.

So turn the page.

Ideas at Imagineering often start with something as simple as a little doodle or a written note. And since Imagineers will do almost anything for a free lunch, many of those ideas are actually scribbled down on napkins—a recurring motif you'll find throughout our journey along The Imagineering Way.

*The limitless possibilities and the
untold dread of a blank piece of paper ...
the unbridled creativity of childhood ...
the unexpected opportunities that spawn
ideas, questions, and answers.
In a world where dreams become realities ...*

The Sky's the Limit

18

John Horny
Concept Designer

The Blank Sheet of Paper

I've been quoted so often on this, it's almost a cliché. But as George Lucas once told us, "Don't avoid the clichés—they are clichés because they work!" So here goes.

There are two ways to look at a blank sheet of paper. One way is to see it as *the most frightening thing in the world* … because when you're faced with that blank page, you must make the first mark on it. It doesn't matter whether you're an artist, a writer, an engineer, or an accountant. Making that first mark is the challenge.

The other way to look at that blank sheet of paper is to see it as *the greatest opportunity in the world.* And for the same reason, but with an important nuance: *you get to make that first mark on that blank sheet!* You can let your imagination fly in any direction. You can create whole new worlds. You can think out of the box.

There's no question that making that first mark can cause even the most lionhearted among us to think twice. Should I play it safe and give the boss what I *think* he/she wants? Or should I be a risk taker and head in a new direction?

We want our Imagineers to be risk takers, willing to strike out in new directions every time they see that blank page. And sometimes that means you *will* strike out. The very best batters in baseball get a hit in only about one third of their at-bats—and grand slams are rare. The National Basketball Association's highest scorers make only 40 percent to 50 percent of their attempts. The best pros know they have to take their swings and shots.

You must go for it, to be a winner!

In my experience outside Imagineering, in community activities and volunteer organizations, a culture of risk taking is a rare thing. Conformity is too often prized as a virtue. Risk my standing on the board of my community organization, church or synagogue, homeowners association, and the like? What will my friends and neighbors say? How will they treat my kids?

That's the dilemma … and I suggest that how you respond to that challenge will speak volumes about who you are and what you accomplish in life.

As Walt Disney told us so often, "Take a chance." I am willing to bet your life will be more exciting, and rewarding, if you see that next blank page, and that next community meeting, as a golden opportunity to step out in new directions.

Why not?

Everything begins somewhere … .

Marty Sklar
Vice Chairman and Principal Creative Executive

When something is so obviously the right thing to do, you can't wait to show it off to someone else.

Good ideas sell themselves. They don't always fund themselves, but they do sell themselves.

Always say "yes" first, then go off and figure it out.

You *Are* Creative. Remember?

No matter what anyone might say to the contrary (including yourself!), you *do* have a creative bone in your body. It's a natural part of your being. Like everyone else on this planet, you were born with the gift of being creative and probably had a joyous time with it until you started to "grow up." That's when you put this gift back in the box, much like a toy you were getting too old to play with. It would be a shame to spend the rest of your life leaving this most precious box—filled with countless dreams and untold surprises—tucked away and unopened!

Children are truly the most creative human beings on the planet. To a child, a chair or sofa can be a ship sailing on a vast sea of carpet. Mud can make a pie. A kitchen pot can be a helmet. A floor lamp can be a monster from outer space that attacks the world with its deadly light ray. A cardboard

wrapping-paper tube can be an enchanted sword. Kids are fearless and free in their thinking and play. Just because you're a grown-up doesn't mean you can't be fearless and free in your creative thinking, too. After all, what is an adult but a child all grown up?

Take a trip down memory lane to your own childhood and tap into the source of your creativity. What a gold mine! You finger-painted with spaghetti sauce. You sculpted exquisite creations out of mashed potatoes and Play-Doh. You saw animal shapes in the clouds. You made up songs and acted out roles and made believe you could fly. You allowed your imagination to take you soaring far beyond physics and logic to a place where you could do everything and be anything in the whole wide universe. You were so creative. Remember?

You still have that childhood imagination, you know. It's just that you began to suppress it when you realized others were judging your unique style of creativity. Someone told you that the purple elephant with the pink polka dots you were painting was silly. Someone told you that the giraffe you saw in the sky was only a stupid cloud. Someone pointed out the real world that existed outside of your imagination. That's when you started to "grow up."

When children grow up, their imaginations certainly go along with them on the road of life, but they take the backseat. The farther people travel this distraction- and opinion-potted road, the farther they get from their sofa ships, construction paper, glue, Play-Doh, and, well, childlike imaginations. If you were to take a little detour along this road and stop at Imagineering, you'd find plenty of construction paper, glue, and clay, and an endless supply of childlike imagination. Imagineers are people who never stopped believing in make-believe. Like Peter Pan, they won't grow up. Why? Because you can only get to Never Land if you believe you can fly.

The kids who create miniature "rides" from shoe boxes, Tinker Toys, and crayons are the same ones who build them for real one day as Imagineers. They are able to dream and do, because, no matter what, they held tightly onto their childhood imagination with all of their might. Imagineers range in age from twenty to ninety-four, but they are all curious kids who believe in the power and pure magic of their imaginations.

When you want to make the most of your creative abilities or rediscover what they are, do what Imagineers do: allow yourself to be a kid again and let the fun and fearlessness of childlike creativity set you free! Untie the ropes of opinion and rejection that are holding your imagination down, so it can soar into the deep blue sky of endless opportunity. Then hop onto that noble purple-and-pink-polka-dotted elephant, face your enemy—fear—with a kitchen-pot helmet and cardboard sword, and charge full speed ahead into that land of countless dreams and untold surprises!

Kevin Rafferty
Senior Show Writer, Director, Creative Development

Don't try and solve a problem too early ... let the problem evolve so you understand it. The stew needs to simmer. Let the idea tell you where it wants to find its own balance.

At Imagineering it's harder to make an idea go away than it is to keep it moving!

Get the problem solved
by saying "try this."
If that doesn't work,
say it again.

Let your creative juices flow, reach for whole new ideas that no one ever thought of or tried to accomplish before. If you aren't the lead dog, the view never changes.

Marty Sklar

The Care and Feeding of the Artistic Soul
—or—
Life among Imagineers as a Pattern for Living

I started with horses at the age of eight, mucking out stalls at a private Saddle Horse show barn in South Meriden, Connecticut. I was way too little and not nearly strong enough to do the job in a timely fashion, but neither the stench of the ammonia-soiled straw, nor the weight of the water buckets deterred me from the joy of being surrounded by those magnificent four-legged creatures.

One mare, Intoxication, would lie down, especially in winter, and let me curl up next to her, using the side of her belly to do my geometry homework. It was cold, but I was always warm enough to get my fingers to move. I remember feeling so safe, in my own world, under the cobwebbed bulb, waiting for my Dad to come to pick me up. And I would draw— huge barns, huge ranches, Intoxication's stall, the barn cats, and her big brown beautiful eyes over and over again. And I would daydream.

I was given riding lessons in exchange for my labor. And it paid off, as the man who owned my beautiful Intoxication gave me hand-me-down show clothes (they were boy's!) and some professional training. By 1962, we were New England Juvenile Five-Gaited Champions. It was my first taste of being the Best. I really liked it.

Years later, when I joined Disney in California, I started riding again—after a fifteen-year absence. My dear friend (and future husband) Frank Armitage had a horse, and encouraged me to take it up again. The passion had never left. So I looked for a teacher. That's how I started in dressage, a French word that simply means "training."

So, while I was learning how to contribute to this Disney way of creating, I was also learning how to teach a horse to carry me more comfortably, with greater expression. In short, to learn how to dance!

The similarities between getting a potentially high-flying creative idea off the stagnant ground, and starting a young horse on the road to a happy life as an elastic, nimble-footed riding partner are more than one would think. As ridiculous as it may sound, both of these major portions of my life have fed each other throughout the years—and provided clues for each other in times of stagnation and stress.

It has often occurred to me that my quest for growth—as an artist, as a professional, and as a rider—has often been confused with a desire to be in control. Concepts of leadership get confused with domination. But in horsemanship, when you aggressively dominate—without listening to feedback—you eventually lose control. Success comes when you can convince the horse to do what you want him to do. And it's not exactly by whispering.

For instance, with a young newborn horse, the instincts for flight are high. He can run with the herd within minutes of being born. It is his survival. Whether he is prey, not predator, depends on how quickly he can run with the herd. This natural instinct is at the core of all progress toward partnership, because first you must have forward motion.

With a newborn horse, you can put the halter on at infancy, and you lead the mother, and the baby sometimes follows. He moves forward, without your even touching him. This is actually so hard for us humans to learn to do. To not control, to not force or coerce—but to work with what is there naturally. Eventually, he moves with you, a hair out in front so that you are at his shoulder.

You don't want to pull, you don't want to get out in front and "lead" by pulling on his head. He'll pull backward. That's the fight instinct. Chances are he could rear up, you might pull against him, and he could cross a leg over the rope, panic, flip himself over, and really hurt himself—or you. And all you've taught him is that you, the leader, are going to corner him into a position where he has to fight. That's coercion.

Confrontation with horses or people either leads to fighting or complete broken submission.

The same is true when you get on him in the beginning months. After he's exhibited being comfortable with the saddle and tack and moving forward with it in an arena, you can ask him to move forward carrying your weight.

You stay out of his way when he's traveling along at a good rhythmic clip and help to rebalance him, with your weight, when he gets unsteady. Pulling, pushing, and yanking on his mouth will only cause fear, make him tense, and shorten his stride. It's just like when you learned to drive—in a large turn, if the car starts fishtailing a little, you ask for a little more forward motion, from behind. That is, step on the gas! With a horse, you make a game out of it. If he bucks or jumps, you go with it. You giggle! He can do no wrong!

The same is so true in the beginning of an Imagineering blue sky session. You have a goal (a new ride, a new methodology, a better ride), but in the beginning, in order for everyone to feel safe about contributing, what is needed is forward motion. And giggling! It doesn't matter in what direction things are moving, just so long as there is forward motion. No judgments allowed. Silly is good. It's a game!

And at this point, leading is not pulling, because people will pull back at the slightest sense of coercion. The energy—when it's successful—comes from behind, from underneath. That's where the ignition is ... in the hind legs! When an idea "has legs," it means that everyone can feel that it's an idea that will support itself. It will "go" somewhere.

What starts to happen is magic, if you think about it. There's an energy, a pulse. Everyone feels it, and excitement starts to build—especially when the mental and emotional connections start. I like to think of it as rhythm. We all instinctively understand and search out rhythm. The young horse running with a rider on its back—you both feel the rhythm, the steady pulse of the different gaits. You are balanced, you are in the groove ... together. It's almost like having wings.

In a room full of unwieldy crazy idea-laden Imagineers, the same emotions arise. The idea, in its own search for becoming, takes on a life of its own. And it's so exciting, this journey, especially when the confines of a specific methodology are left for later. What pops up along the way is sometimes a better idea. It's a herd of creative energy, and when it's right, everyone wants to join the dance.

Dr. Ross Edy, a well-known international neuro-scientist and longtime friend of my husband, once told me that if you take two separate live heart cells from two separate mammals and put them pulsing in the same petri dish—left alone—in a short time, they will find each other's rhythm and start to beat in time with each other. How profound is that!

Rhythm played an enormous part in my extended family. My brother-in-law George, as a teenager, had a baby sister who was born with Down's syndrome. At five years old, Liz still had not walked. George loved his pounding rock and roll, and spent much of his time gyrating around to the music. Liz, who so wanted to jump and jive with her brother, started bouncing up and down to the music—in rhythm! So, George would balance her on top of his feet, and they would "dance to the music." Through this dancing, on top of her brother's feet, her muscles got stronger, her lower back got supple and strong, she got balance—and learned to walk! By dancing to the rhythm!

So now we have created the forward motion, and we have discovered the inherent rhythm. Now we need to find a little direction.

With a colt, it is guiding him into a perfect circle, first to the left and then to the right. But you don't do it by pulling on the side of his mouth that you want him to turn. You build a wall on his outside, with your leg, your upper thigh, the weight of your seat, and finally in a steady contact, your outside hand, which is connected to his mouth, and he will move away from it. Basically, you are just closing the door on the direction that you don't want him to go in—all the while maintaining the rhythm and the forward.

And practice and wait. Patience. Everyone wants quick results. Horses can only learn one thing at a time. I've often wondered whether that's also true about us as humans. I sense that we can only practice one thing at a time until it becomes second nature. How often it has occurred to me that team/idea dynamics seem to build when everyone is comfortable with one another. But that's because there is a familiarity already established. Time has passed, they know each other, they already understand and trust the mental dynamics. With the colt it is physical; with a group of people in search of a concept, it's free association. And the pace and rhythm can intensify when everyone's in sync. But first it takes patience.

Soon flexibility arrives. As the horse gets stronger over the years, the circles can become smaller, and eventually he will learn to move sideways—all the while learning to keep his back, upon which you sit, supple and relaxed. You, as leader, should always be there, to provide the trust that if he gets out of rhythm, out of balance, he can go back to you for the security of the rhythm and the balance.

And there are mistakes that are made. I've made many. With horses and people. And I have to say that it's been mostly about breaking trust. Not about getting out of rhythm or out of balance, or trying to coerce and dominate. It's been about not being honest with myself about what is not working. Horses carry no grudges. They have pain and fear memory, but no mental grudges. They have no hidden agendas, so they can be a perfect mirror. They reflect back to you the dynamics of the relationship you have established. So many times I have asked myself, "What am I doing that is getting in the way of what I want to happen?"

I have found that question and the honest answers so helpful in my Imagineering life also. It's trickier, because as humans with powers of cognitive reasoning, we build perceptions that govern our behavior. And thus we can easily fall victim to harboring hidden agendas. I have found that the issues of control, power, and dominance surround us daily. But in learning from my horses, I have learned that I, too, give my best, and behave at my best when I feel supported from underneath and not mentally abused.

So I've learned that it's that simple concept that I must consistently impart to those with whom I work. My horses have shown me that not holding a grudge can be liberating. And they have taught me to build my own belief in people, based on visible results of their consistent behavior pattern, not in what they say about who they are. And ultimately my horses have taught me that my own behavior must match my words and be consistent. And rhythmic. And there's that rhythm thing again.

A beautiful horse, like a beautiful idea, has its own being. I've learned that, as humans, we can mold, shape, and develop—either through patient discipline of our own mental, spiritual, and physical selves or by loudly calling attention to ourselves.

But in the end, the natural beauty of the horse, the brilliance of an idea, the creation of a concept have their own power, regardless of where the original seed came from.

My big and beautiful and powerful happy horses have allowed me to learn that to be a custodian in partnership with that energetic beauty, as opposed to perceiving myself as creator, has unlocked a journey that has far surpassed anything I could ever do on my own.

Karen Connolly Armitage
Senior Concept Designer
Creative Development

Any one thing can move a company.
It's the quality of the idea that counts.
I've been surprised how many times over
the years little creative ideas
have grown into something *big*.

Michael Eisner

Chairman and CEO, The Walt Disney Company

Never fall in love with your idea
because it will change tomorrow.

Enjoy the process—enjoy the change.

Gather, Store, and Recombine

In creating the original Journey Into Imagination for Epcot, we pondered for nearly six months just what comprised the process of imagination. Was there a basic process in common that held true for both a major scientific breakthrough and a beautifully decorated birthday cake?

Indeed, we discovered, there is. Everyone goes through a process of gathering information, storing it, and recombining it with other thoughts to produce something new.

Just as you are gathering information from this book and storing it in your mind, you may later recall the ideas you have stored to aid in the creation of something new. A scientist, an artist, or a parent creating that special birthday cake use exactly the same process.

In the twenty years since our discovery, after working on countless creative projects at work and at home, I have been hard pressed to find a creation of imagination—simple or profound—that hasn't resulted from this process.

Tony Baxter

Senior Vice President, Creative Development

The Bunny Story

When you're trying to sell an idea, whether it's to your boss, a spouse, your family, or some friends, you might think of your audience as a little bunny rabbit hiding in the bushes, just out of reach, its nose twitching, sniffing the air, sensing food, and fearing danger.

You want that bunny rabbit to feast on your idea, but first you have to coax him out from under the bushes and convince him it's safe to take a little nibble.

So think of your idea as a sweet, crunchy carrot.

The bunny rabbit needs to perceive a safe, non-threatening environment, as well as a reward that will justify the risk it's taking by poking its head out.

Remember that any sudden movement or loud noise is going to scare the bunny away. And don't hold out a carrot that's too big. In fact, you might think of the carrot as just a portion of your idea, rather than the entire concept.

It's a carrot topping to a whole salad of ideas.

When a concept is revolutionary and changes the current thinking or status quo (no matter how much you know in your heart it's the right thing to do), a big change can be a scary thing for someone to try to take in all at once. If you were trying to coax the bunny out so it could feast on an entire salad, you wouldn't dump the whole salad on the ground at one time. The bunny would disappear back into its office—er, rabbit hole—before the last piece of lettuce floated to the ground.

Just coax it out gently with a tasty sample of what's to come, then carefully introduce the benefits of the big picture: your salad.

Sometimes, after the first nibble, the bunny will still disappear down its hole, but if it liked the carrot well enough, and didn't sense too much danger outside the bushes, chances are the bunny will be back before you know it, ready to take on the whole salad.

Bruce Gordon
Project Director
Creative Development

How to Be an Artist

You can't imagine how many times someone has said to me, "I wish I was an artist, but I just never had any talent." Hogwash! The skills of art can be learned just like anything else.

So why do some people seem to be more talented than others? In my opinion, artists need one and only one thing: *belief in themselves*. If you think you are an artist, and have confidence in that fact, then all you need to do is learn how to do it. Simple as that.

No more excuses! If you truly want to be an artist, *be one*. Find a pen or pencil that you like, and draw on everything. Well, maybe not on everything, but on things that won't get you in trouble. Doodling is endlessly entertaining.

Stop worrying about what you are trying to achieve and just start sketching. You will be astonished at what comes out of your head. And one of these days someone may even pay you to have fun! It's the greatest feeling in the world.

Chuck **Chuck Ballew**

Senior Concept Designer, Creative Development

The Value of Ideas, Part I

We always hear about how we should never get attached to specific ideas, because the creative process is all about freedom, openness, and broad thinking. There are a lot of tools to promote that, entire books devoted to "the art of the brainstorm," "keeping fresh," and so on. It is, of course, important not to get attached to a concept, and limit the flow of ideas. However, a little too often that adds up to making ideas "cheap." Playing devil's advocate, I would like to make a case for "valuing" ideas.

Idea vs. Logic

Strong fundamental ideas are not necessarily bulletproof; they may not resurface or endure on their own strength and merits. They are often so simple that they are difficult to articulate. A lot of times the only immediate argument you come up with is "Because it looks cool." Your gut tells you it's strong—not so much your logic.

It's easy to start talking yourself out of a good idea. Groups are especially good at that: the members start talking about all the reasons, questions, or unknowns about a concept and start forgetting what was so strong about it in the first place. Keeping that purity of the first idea is pretty hard through the process. All stories and designs require an internal logic, but the logic can evolve, too.

My note to self: "If you find your logic is talking you out of a good idea, question the logic first, then question the idea. This is entertainment: logic is less important than the impact of the story and design."

Truly good fundamental ideas are also few and far between. We really have to watch for them. They are often drowned out in the noise of off-the-cuff thoughts, quotes, or solutions.

Idea vs. Solution

There is a difference between an idea and a solution. In my mind an idea drives fundamental aspects of stories and environments, while solutions are responses to situations or requirements. Sometimes specific people are better at one than the other, but the two are not mutually exclusive.

What happens a lot, though, is confusing a solution for an idea. As projects progress, they naturally require more and more solutions and fewer and fewer fundamental ideas. When a fundamental concept is introduced in the middle of a project, everyone gets energized, because it's a rare event. In the beginning, what we look for are the ideas, themes, and story points that will drive future choices. Only true "blue sky" lets you ignore conditions, and play the "what if?" scenarios fully.

However, most projects start with some requirements in theme, programming, and budget. This show has to fit here, or cost this much, be done by this date, or use this property. When we start there, we are already partially in the realm of solutions. I find it a good idea in that case to check as I go whether the ideas that are coming up will be driving the rest of the project or whether the early requirements will be driving it through the idea.

The guests only experience the story/environment/ride as it was invented and executed; they do not value the reasons why the attraction got done.

When we're lucky, a concept is both a great idea and a great solution.

My note to self: "Try to remember how/why an idea showed up—don't confuse a solution for an idea; value an idea for its power to drive many choices down the line and to satisfy the guests' expectation."

Luc Mayrand
Concept Designer

The "idea" is held in such high regard here, and therefore, so are the people who come up with those ideas. We cherish the dreamers, misfits, and oddballs who populate our hallways.

Christian Hope
Concept Design Director,
Creative Development

Every new project at Imagineering starts with the assumption that it will be fun and exciting. We never say we don't really want to do it this way—we do it the best way we know how. We are our end users because we like the product.

Everything I learned in life, I learned at Walt Disney Imagineering

Okay, that's a bit of an overstatement. They didn't teach me how to make French toast. I learned that in high school. But much of what I know about creativity, I learned over my formative years (ages 30–40) here in this wildly creative atmosphere known as Walt Disney Imagineering. Over the years, I have picked up some wonderful life lessons that I'm going to share with you now … whether you like it or not.

Don't be afraid of visual aids. Sure, you can sell your idea with words alone, but why would you? Remember the old adage "a picture is worth a thousand words"? Well, after adjustment for inflation, I would put that at about 1.5 million words per picture. So, do yourself a favor and give your audience some visual references. Even if you aren't artistically inclined and cannot find an artist to save your life—go ahead and draw stick figures, build a model out of matchsticks, make shadow puppets—in short, do anything that will get your idea across visually to your audience!

Keep your ears open. A good idea can come from anyone. Walt Disney used to solicit the custodians for their opinions because he knew that everyone has the capacity to be creative—only a rare few actually get paid for it. Hey, I've even heard some great ideas come from Finance people. Really.

Blue sky has nothing to do with the Weather Channel. It has everything to do with freedom from failure. In a blue-sky session, there is no such thing as a bad idea. The word "no" is never uttered. I have never felt such freedom since I was in preschool. Go ahead and hold a blue-sky meeting over anything: what color to paint the break room … what everyone should wear on Fridays. Blue sky works for anything.

When you're stuck, take a walk. Get out of your office and find someone—anyone—and talk to him or her about anything … anything except your idea. With any luck, the other person is also working on an idea and will want to bounce it off you and get your input. Sometimes thinking about something else is just what your brain needs to get it unstuck. This leads directly to my next point:

Some of the most productive meetings occur nowhere near a conference room. Here at Imagineering we have what is known as a corridor culture. No, it's not something that needs to be removed by emergency technicians in hazmat suits. Corridor culture promotes impromptu meetings in the hallways, around the water cooler, by the coffee machine, even in the bathroom. Just remember to wash your hands after that meeting.

Never underestimate the power of a stack of multicolored index cards. I've been in brainstorms with them and I've been in brainstorms without them, and believe me, you want those cards … you need those cards. Preferably with a bucket full of felt-tipped markers nearby. Sometimes a doodle on an index card has advanced an idea further than mere yakking around a conference table ever could. Then, make sure you pin those cards to the wall or a storyboard or something. You can judge a brainstorming session by how many cards are plastered on the wall at the end of the meeting. Which brings me to my next point:

Blank walls are your enemy! The only time you see an empty wall at Imagineering is when it's being repainted. We like our walls covered with artwork and photographs, thank you very much. All the better to inspire creative thinking.

If all else fails, make yourself some French toast. Again, not something I learned at Imagineering, but if you need a good recipe, why not have a brainstorming session? Ask someone in the hallway. Have a blue-sky meeting. "Does it *have* to be French toast? What's wrong with a bagel? How about French-toasted bagels?"

Steve Spiegel
Senior Show Writer, Theme Park Productions

IMAGINEERING THE OCEAN

Vast, deeply hypnotic, bleak, embracing and enticing, reflecting agitation or calm, blue or gray. At Imagineering, creation is in constant motion. Lessons are a rhythm of continuous ideas approaching, waves passing, the promise of others, and vigilant, strained awareness with gleaming tools in anticipation. Imagineers are alert, hungry, frosty, sharp, searching for idea ripples at all times, ready to construct inner creations in our Parks and Resorts.

Paul Comstock
Landscape Architect

Ask the Right Questions

Whether you're soliciting help from others or tackling the challenge yourself, you must first be able to articulate what the challenge is—otherwise, how will you be able to choose the best path to resolution?

Articulating a challenge requires you to let go of all the possible solutions you are considering and pare the challenge back to its core. What is the bare essence of the challenge in front of you?

The example we use at Imagineering Research & Development is that someone has asked you to make a fan for them. If we didn't know better, off we'd go to make a fan (it'd be the best fan in the world ... full of features no one would ever expect, but a fan nonetheless). But since we're enlightened about the creative process of approaching challenges, we ask questions first. Inevitably, our questions reveal that what the person really wants is to be cool. They assumed a fan was the only or best solution. But in doing so, they run the risk of never hearing alternative solutions, such as a window that opens, an air conditioner, or even, perhaps, a fan.

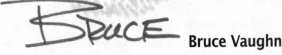

Bruce Vaughn

Executive Director, Research & Development

Password Three

Each time someone challenges me with a blank sheet of paper, I'm overcome by an uncontrollable urge to wrap his next gift in it.

I have the good fortune of being third in a queue of four offspring. Three was always my favorite number. Being third afforded me the opportunity to develop, in the family rumpus room, the core of my skills as a manager of amazing Imagineers. I am still an avid practitioner of those skills today. They work. Other peripheral, but useful, knowledge is explained in detail in the paragraph above. There is more exposition about my obsession with the number three below.

Until recently, there was a three in my computer password as well. Unfortunately, they ran out of things called three sometime last summer—August, I think it was. I reluctantly switched to four. Four turns out to be a good number. My younger brother George is the fourth in that offspring queue— the creative force in the family. I always wrap his gifts in blank paper. I have for years. He needs all the blank sheets of paper he can lay his hands on.

"Blank sheets, if taken," I say, "must always be returned full." He smiles, his eyes sparkle, and he's off. He knows that blank sheets rarely fall prey to the shredder and therefore are seldom in short supply, but still he has an insatiable need for them. It's a mystery to me. I have no interest in solving it. Something I learned long ago, in the rumpus room.

When I didge up in the morning, I still reach, with my left-hand ring finger, for that three key that was for too long a part of my password. Old habits die hard. When I catch myself, I print out three blank sheets. There are always new gifts to wrap and amazing Imagineers to manage.

Mike Morris

Vice President, Theatrical Design and Production

Growing a Culture

... with mentoring and teamwork ...
enthusiasm and passion ...
stimulation and motivation ...
storytelling and communication ...
all the elements in our petri dish of creativity.

If I have seen further than others, it is because I was standing on the shoulders of giants.
—*Isaac Newton*

Every Sorcerer Was Once an Apprentice

I could not believe it.

There I was, sitting with Disney Legend Wathel Rogers, having a wonderful conversation about the origins of Audio-Animatronics figures. It seemed surreal to me.

I mean, I was just this newly hired, lowly 19-year-old apprentice Imagineer, and here was the "grandfather" of Disney's Audio-Animatronics technology taking the time to talk to me and patiently answer my barrage of questions.

I really can't remember much about the specifics of what we talked about during that first day we met in person, as I was in a kind of light-headed, giddiness-induced fog. However, I do remember that I was happy beyond what words can describe at being able to finally meet the man who had been such an important mentor to me during my quest to become an Imagineer.

I first came to know Wathel through our correspondence as "pen pals." When I was around 14 or so, I instantly knew that I had found my calling after seeing Pirates of the Caribbean for the first time while on a family vacation. I got the wild idea in my head to try to build an Audio-Animatronics figure. About a year later, after I had completed my first animatronic parrot and programming system in my garage, Marty Sklar received a newspaper article about me and forwarded it on to several Imagineers, including Wathel, who then sent me a wonderful introductory letter.

For the next few years, I frequently sent Wathel letters that updated my progress as I built several more figures and programming systems. His responding letters were usually filled with his own questions, which got me thinking about how I could improve what I had done, or how to solve a technical problem I was having. "What if you tried doing this?" he would often reply.

He gave me invaluable suggestions as to where I could find tidbits of information about Disney's Audio-Animatronics systems to help me piece it all together. One of the great tips he gave me was about some detailed pictures of the mechanism inside the head of Disney's first animated Abraham Lincoln figure in an old *National Geographic* magazine.

What was so amazing to me was that he had a genuine interest in what I was attempting to do, and took the time to encourage, support, and guide me. He could have ignored my letters, but he didn't. He could have sent me a cold, impersonal form letter explaining that everything that I wanted to know was proprietary, but he didn't. He could have told me that he was too busy to help, and that I should stop bothering him, but he didn't. He could have been critical, negative, or pessimistic about my chances of becoming an Imagineer, but he wasn't.

I could have given up many times out of frustration when I hit a dead end or a technical snag, but I didn't, because Wathel chose to be my mentor.

After I completed building my most complex animatronic parrot and control system, my childhood dream came true and I was given the opportunity of a nine-month trial apprenticeship at Imagineering.

A short time after the start of my apprenticeship, Wathel, who was recovering from an illness at the time, returned to work. When we finally met in person I felt as though we were like old friends with a long history. I remember his smiling, extending his hand, and saying, "Good job and welcome aboard."

For the next several months that he continued to work before finally retiring, I used every opportunity I had to talk with him and to learn from his inspirational stories. The memories and experiences he generously shared with me, in a way, have now become my own.

His history has become a part of my history.

Similar mentoring relationships, and the creation of the legacies produced by them, are a cultural tradition that I think is unique to Imagineering. While it can't be said that my own experiences are typical of anyone else's, I believe that there are countless other stories of mentoring relationships between veteran Imagineers and their apprentices.

As I continue to fulfill my childhood dream as an Imagineer today, I can't help but try to be a mentor to others wherever and whenever I can. I believe it's the highest honor I can give to all of my past and present mentors at Imagineering, especially Wathel Rogers.

Steve "Mouse" Silverstein
Principal Developer, Animation Programming Systems
Show Animation and Programming

Walt Disney continues to mentor all of us, through the stories we hear and read about him. Walt believed in the generosity, optimism, and the goodness of human beings. Mentoring involves giving, the need to respect people and embrace the bond of humans.

As a mentor, don't provide every answer. Rather, ask "Why do you think it is this way?" A good mentor doesn't give the answers, but helps others figure it out for themselves.

Chuck Ballew
Senior Concept Designer
Creative Development

Teamwork at Imagineering

Early in my career with Disney, we were trying to finish the kid's play area at the Old Key West Resort at Walt Disney World. The contractor had just finished the icon structure—a big sand castle—and it looked terrible!

Jim Durham, who was working on the project with me, remembered that John Hench was in town, and suggested we beg him to come over and give us some advice. I had never met John, but had, of course, heard of his great reputation as the Imagineering "design guru." Jim and I were not officially Imagineers at the time—we worked for the Disney Development Company—but John did come by to see us. After a bit, he took out his sketch pad and drew us a quick drawing to give to the contractor, along with some advice on colors. And that's how we fixed the problem.

I learned then that you are never alone at Imagineering. No matter how difficult the problem, there is always someone who has seen worse and who knows just what to do. Since then, I've never hesitated to ask for help when I've needed it, and I've always gotten it enthusiastically. We work as a team at Imagineering, and that's how problems get solved.

Don Goodman
President, Walt Disney Imagineering

Thinking outside the box can lead to all sorts of new discoveries and perspectives, but sometimes—when faced with tight budgets and schedules—thinking inside the box can be just as rewarding.

My Introduction to Imagineering Happened at Church

Epic concepts like locust plagues, oceans parting, and men riding fiery chariots can be hard to grasp, and sometimes the mind wanders. That's what was happening when I spotted the Imagineer a few rows in front of me. Even though it was Sunday mass, he was wearing a black leather jacket with the Sorcerer Mickey logo and the words "Walt Disney Imagineering" emblazoned on the back. It was unorthodox, it was original, it was … cool.

Being a high school student in Orlando at the time and not having much experience with the corporate ladder, I pulled him aside, and boldly asked him what his job was and how he had gotten it. It was clear to me that any job worth advertising on your back in church seemed like a good career path.

This Imagineer, and engineer by trade, dealt kindly with my barrage of questions (no doubt hoping that would be the end of it). But as if being corralled outside his house of worship and pestered about Disney's long-term development plans weren't enough, I threw him a curveball.

"How can I get a job with Imagineering?"

Since I wasn't yet entrusted with a driver's license, being entrusted with guests' personal safety and hard-earned vacations wasn't gonna happen. But I did get the next best thing: he invited me to spend a day at the parks with these mysterious Imagineers.

It was the ultimate scam, I figured: while my peers sat through another mundane day in the classroom, I found myself on a man-made mountain—Splash Mountain—overlooking the swampy lowlands of central Florida.

I had the whole thing to myself. Well, I shared it with a few ride engineers, but at six in the morning, there was not a single tourist to be seen.

On the edge of the ride's legendary plunge, one of the Imagineers gave the word for the water to be turned on. In a split second, an impressive torrent of water cascaded through the mountain, tumbling into the briar patch below.

Back in church soon thereafter, the parting of the Red Sea somehow seemed much more believable.

Phil Guidry

Creative Development, Theme Park Productions

**The anonymity of creativity—
sometimes, no one knows your name!**

When we fail, we don't stop. Sometimes you have to go backward in order to go forward, but we never stop.

It's important that you own an idea, for without an owner there's no way to move an idea forward. But it's equally important that you not be possessive about it. When people own an important work of art, they have a sense of stewardship rather than possession.

To be an Imagineer, it's important to keep reality at arm's length.

Christian Hope, Concept Design Director
Creative Development

Maintain the ability to adapt. Be passionate about your idea but be able to adapt to what you find out along the way. Don't go down fighting every time!

Our Graffiti Culture

Now, we don't recommend you follow *all* the advice we give in this book—and a case in point is a little solution we came up with for an interior-decorating challenge.

In 1990, the local fire marshal made a visit to Imagineering's headquarters in Glendale, California. Our main building is an eclectic mix of offices, studios, work spaces, conference rooms, crafts shops, and storage areas. In the back half of the building is a warehouse-sized room where we build our larger models. The fire marshal informed us that we needed to construct an emergency egress corridor along one side of this massive room that would run from one side of the building to the other.

Soon enough, we had a nine-foot by nine-foot passageway, with a concrete floor and walls and ceiling made of pressboard, that stretched the length of the building, about four hundred feet. It was very long, and very bland. Not surprisingly, Imagineers do not like bland. Vice chairman and principal creative executive Marty Sklar made a suggestion: why don't Imagineers decorate the walls in their own inimitable fashion?

We're not talking a nice coat of Navajo white with colorful accents here and there. What the Imagineers had in mind was something far more personal, eccentric, and, well, just uniquely Imagineering.

Well, early on a Wednesday morning in 1990, hundreds of Imagineers descended on the hallway and wrote and drew on the walls. They painted castles, drew portraits, wrote stories, sketched self-deprecating cartoons, and, in one case, thanked Walt (that would be Walt Disney) for giving them the opportunity to have this much fun—and get paid to do it.

Today, the Graffiti Hallway endures. And thrives. Imagineers still leave their imprints when the mood moves them, and it's become a rite of passage for college interns to make their mark somewhere along the corridor.

Perhaps that's our next challenge: how to preserve this graffiti and still move on. When remodeling endangered one of our graffiti sketches of Marty himself, the art was extracted from the wall, literally—the paint, the pressboard, and the two-by-four framing studs—all of it deposited in Marty's office.

Not a real practical solution for an entire hallway, but stay tuned—we may yet invent the answer!

Dave Fisher
Senior Show Writer, Creative Development

Creating Visions

"Hearing something five hundred times
is not as good as seeing it once."
—*Chinese Proverb*

The success of the Walt Disney Company has centered on two basic and fundamental concepts: our ability to be great storytellers, and the constant and the vigilant search for exciting new ideas. Two concepts that not only drive this company but are the building blocks for all successful enterprises.

At first glance, storytelling is about the scripts and characters developed for the various shows and attractions. However, most of our "stories" are told without words at all! Since Disney theme parks are about fantastic places and spaces, most of the time the story has to be told by the place itself.

A walk into an elegant and simple past is seen on Main Street, U.S.A., an excursion into the future can be experienced in Tomorrowland, and a trip into the exotic ports of the world can be enjoyed in Adventureland. All of these places must communicate to our guests on all levels, from the look of the place to the sounds, down to the smallest details. Our guests are the camera lens by which they are convinced that they have been taken to a new and unique place.

What is the most effective way of telling a story and making ides come to life? Create a vision. Human beings are programmed to believe what they see. If an image conveys the right emotional connection, is accurate in its detail and color, and, in general, pleases the audience it is communicating with, then you have a great chance of selling it.

Movies, architecture, theater, automobiles, interior design, industrial design, television production, computer games, the entire world of science fiction, anything which is driven by ideas and innovation must be communicated in the language of design—art and imagery. Today, there are more opportunities for creating images than ever. Computer-generated images, SimWorlds, storyboarding, image montages, and digital photography are just a few of the examples of bringing vision to ideas.

One doesn't need to be an artist to create visions—one just needs to have ideas and to know that to get them created, they must be put in a form that stimulates and motivates those who are looking for a vision to follow.

Tim Delaney
Vice President, Executive Designer, Creative Development

Imagineering: the Mirror

Wake up, wipe your eyes, and look where the private self is viewed by curious Imagineer brothers and sisters.

Look, undressed, where, being the best in their fields, they are scanning to see, listen, react, and evaluate that most personal possession: your naked ideas.

The Imagineering mirror forces us to know ourselves. By knowing ourselves, we can contribute to the team collaboration and the vision is built.

The Imagineering Team collaboration is the mirror vision of our creative images.

Paul Comstock

Director of Landscape Design,
Landscape Architects

The world belongs to the dogged, the persistent, and the passionate. And to have that kind of persistence, you need to be in love with the idea. Learn all about it, so you can find what there is to love about it. Love the material, make it your own.

Before you can plant a garden, you've got to have the dirt. But you don't have to be in love with the dirt—you're in love with what the landscape will look like when it's done. You're passionate about what the dirt will allow you to accomplish.

Invite the voices that never get heard. The passion needs to come from everybody.

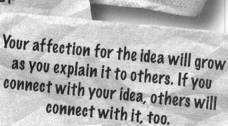

Your affection for the idea will grow as you explain it to others. If you connect with your idea, others will connect with it, too.

The joy should be in doing the work—the reward is hoping the guests enjoy our efforts.

David Mumford
Imagineer

Tell a Story

Solving a challenge, no matter what it is, involves telling a story. So, when Imagineers begin a new project, we tell one another stories. When you tell someone a story, chances are they'll tell more stories back to you, and your idea will grow and evolve, as it never could have on its own. There's an internal logic that grows out of storytelling.

We communicate our stories in ride adventures like Pirates of the Caribbean, or visually through architecture like Sleeping Beauty Castle or Space Mountain, or through one-of-a-kind 3-D films like *It's Tough to Be a Bug*, and of course, through our Audio-Animatronics animated three-dimensional characters.

In contrast to moviemaking storytelling, the storytelling on our rides is more like advertising, a sort of "shorthand," that delivers lots of information in a short period of time. But our stories and characters have to be just as rewarding.

In Dinoland at Disney's Animal Kingdom, we tell our guests about dinosaurs and paleontology by first inventing a history for our place. We populated the land with characters we came to know and love, making decisions about every element, based on what our characters might have done. The process is shared by the entire team—architects, engineers, model builders, landscape designers, and show designers.

In our invented story, we went all the way back to the 1940s when Chester and Hester bought a small gas station in rural Florida. Chester, an amateur paleontologist, found some dinosaur bones that he shared with his friend, a paleontologist named Dr. Erwin Miller. This simple discovery sets into motion a whole cast of characters who eventually, over the years, come to populate and build what our guests see today as Dinoland.

Stories like Chester and Hester's influenced every decision we made. I really came to love the place we invented and all the characters that live there. But what I really loved was the spirit of all the people I worked with and who made it all come to life.

Our creativity is powerful because it is fueled by all of the team members living together in the worlds we invent—worlds that our guests can come to and live in by discovering all the storytelling details all the Imagineers include in everything they do.

Ann Malmlund
Senior Show Producer/Director, Creative Development

The Wrath of Me

When I received an invitation to contribute to this book, many interesting things to write about popped into my head … but then the realization hit me that by doing so, I would be incurring my own wrath!

Before you think I'm crazy (or maybe you'll think I'm even crazier), I should explain that I have been an in-house lawyer at Imagineering for more than thirteen years, and helping to maintain the confidentiality that surrounds much of what Imagineering does is part of my job.

I doubt that there are many other lawyers who might spend a day poring through technical drawings of some amazing new contraption, discussing copyright law with an artist, negotiating a contract to build giant cartoon figures, and then having a telephone conversation about construction contracting strategy in another part of the world.

One thing that is required is the mind-set that there is always a way to do something—one just has to look hard enough to find it!

Peter Steinman
General Counsel, Walt Disney Imagineering

IMAGINEERING HAIKU:

"Pull out all the stops.

It will always be de-scoped.

No one hears your screams."

Steve Noceti
Principal Scope Writer, Project Estimating

My father often asked me: "Do you want to be right or do you want to be happy?"

To which I would now reply: "An Imagineer would manage to be both."

Creative Systems Analyst, Information Services
Ron Collins

Fermenting a Figment

The right kind of environment can encourage all kinds of creativity. The designers revel in this and have decorated their work spaces according to their own individual muses—from jazz pad to pineapple palace—whatever inspires and feeds the imagination is the order of the day.

Because so much creative discussion happens over lunch, it follows that the design of our cafeterias should inspire food for thought as well. One such dining room was given the tantalizing moniker of "Figment Café"—named after the clever little purple dragon from the Journey into Imagination attraction at Epcot.

Unfortunately, there was nothing very Figmenty about the new eating facility. It had bare white walls and a drab, blocked-in patio populated by exceedingly plain tables and chairs. Even the carpet was gray. This new cafeteria inspired us all right—it inspired us to want to change it immediately.

We envisioned a Discoverers' Club, decorated in a lush Victorian style with exotic props and potted palms. There would be colorful rugs underfoot, and adventurers' maps on the walls. Presiding over it all would be a stylish portrait of Figment, decked out in his designer khakis and sporting an explorer's pith helmet.

The main drawback to our recipe? We had more ambition than budget. When Management threw down the "I don't think you can do it" gauntlet we got a little steamed, but we love a challenge, so we kicked the creative Cuisinart into higher gear.

We sneaked in design-drawing time whenever we could—a dash here and a pinch there. We worked at home on custom decorations. The carpentry shop provided some architectural ornamentation to spice up the drab walls. The team had a weekend painting party, and we all showed up with families in tow to wield paintbrushes (and eat free ice cream).

Finally, the day arrived for our grand unveiling. An excited crowd gathered (free ice cream again!), commemorative buttons were passed out, and congratulatory speeches were made. A lot of personal free time had been donated by everyone, proving that you can accomplish a lot with just a few ingredients, as long as teamwork is at the top of your recipe.

Larry Nikolai
Senior Conceptual Designer, Creative Development

Childish Things

Most people put away their childish things when they grow up. But before you put them all away, consider this story.

Five years ago, Imagineers were given an interesting assignment: to imagine and build a theme park about California—in California! A secret conference room was quickly outfitted with the usual tools of the Imagineering trade: large, easel-sized pads of paper on which to scribble stream-of-consciousness thinking, Magic Markers of every color, and tissue paper—lots and lots of rolls of tissue paper.

"What if … " The room fell quiet. Those two magic words can instantly rivet the attention of an entire room full of Imagineers. All eyes turned toward the speaker. "What if," he continued, "we could fly our guests over the entire state of California without ever leaving the theme park?"

Experience the beauty and majesty of the Golden State from the air, feel the wind on your face, and smell the orange groves and the evergreens. It would have to be a film experience—even Imagineers know they can't move space and time (yet). We would place a huge motion-picture screen below the guests so they could fly over the breathtaking images of California.

"How?" came a lone voice of reason, crying out in the wilderness of imagination. "Well, we'll just take a camera up in an airplane and film the scenes." "No, I mean, how will we, you know, make them *fly*?"

Then we did what we always do in situations like that. We called the "ride guys"—our name for the division of Imagineering called Ride Mechanical Engineering. They've all been to universities that have "Tech" and "Polytechnic" in the title, belong to engineering societies, and, to be perfectly truthful, a few of them *do* wear pocket protectors.

But they also prove one very large truth about imagination: you don't have to go to art school, wear outrageous outfits, and be flamboyant to have imagination. You just have to be intrigued by words like "what if" and "how." And you have to understand the value of "childish things."

Which brings us to Mark Sumner, one of the "ride guys" called in to work out the logistics of this new flying experience.

Mark sketched up several possible solutions, but the geometry of how it would work was going to be difficult to explain on paper. Then Mark remembered he had an old Erector Set in the attic, something he had kept since he was a kid—Erector Set 10211, the Cape Canaveral Set.

After a couple of hours of assembly, augmenting the Erector pieces with some string, hot melt glue, and toilet-paper rolls, a working model materialized. Turn the crank, and the seats left a flat floor and soared up into their positions above the screen.

Mark brought the Erector Set model to the next team meeting in a brown paper grocery bag. "Not saying a word," Mark remembers, "I lifted it out, set it on the table, and turned the crank. In the span of about three seconds, everyone, every discipline, understood the concept. No drawings, no long explanations, no engineering jargon."

Today, the ride system on Soarin' Over California at Disney's California Adventure operates exactly like that model. Sometimes all it takes is remembering how to be a child.

Pam Fisher
Senior Show Writer, Creative Development

Teamwork:
Bouncing Ideas Off One Another
for a Slam Dunk

Casting for a Team

Good casting really begins with self-awareness. The first step is to recognize your own strengths and weaknesses. For instance, if you know you're not very good at casting people, then do yourself a favor and get to know someone who is. Also, be big enough to accept the fact that you're probably very good at certain kinds of tasks, but probably stink at others.

Next, you have to be able to identify strengths and weaknesses in other people. Make mental notes whenever you're with a friend. If a particular friend is good at making mixed music CDs, he or she probably has a good sense of storytelling and pacing. Someone who dresses well also probably can advise you on what gifts or clothes to buy for special occasions.

Also be realistic about how much time a task will take and how much time you truthfully have to dedicate to that task. You may be an excellent cook, but if you have to be in a meeting or on a plane when you should be cooking for a dinner party, hire a chef (or cancel that boring meeting!). Getting the right group together to tackle a challenge is the most effective way to actually overcome any challenge. A well-cast team will succeed where others fail.

Remember that personality quirks, even very strange ones, can often become strengths on a team. And if you don't have a team that supports each other with a single vision, you might wind up with a project that's only okay rather than fantastic.

There's a little story I read as a child that sticks with me to this day. It speaks volumes about learning how to "read" people. There are two barbers in a small, isolated town. One barber's shop is littered with hair all over the floor. His own hair is a mess and he appears to be disorganized. The other barber's shop is clean and well organized. His hair is neat and looks nice. Which barber do you go to for a haircut?

Working only from the information given above, you'd be wise to go to the unkempt barber with the messy shop. Being that the town is small and isolated, one can safely assume he gets his hair cut by the barber with the clean shop, whose shop is probably so organized because he doesn't get much business. Not to mention, his hair is neat and looks nice ... probably the handiwork of the only other barber in town—the messy one.

Bruce **Bruce Vaughn**

Executive Director, Research & Development

Casting for Success

For Imagineers, the opening of a new attraction or theme park is akin to "opening night" for a theatrical production. Our opening night is the moment when the first guests stream through the turnstiles. Success can be measured in terms of smiles and the speed of the initial "mad rush" to be the first in line.

Successful Imagineering opening nights can be traced directly back to teams who were driven by relentless dedication to the product—often strong and diverse groups of people who managed to operate as a single "entity," not an "assemblage of individuals." The most successful teams set, and carefully nurtured, a working environment where affixing blame was unimportant, and victories/defeats were shared uniformly across discipline boundaries.

The continuing challenge at Imagineering is to put as much attention on construction and maintenance of our teams as we do on the physical construction and maintenance of the attractions themselves.

Paul Adams
Director, Project Architecture and Engineering Management

What I've learned in all my years at Imagineering: concepts come and go. Projects turn on and off. Attractions open and close. But relationships built on a foundation of trust and respect—for one another, as well as our guests—will always define the difference between success and failure.

Mike West
Senior Show Producer-Director, Creative Development

I think the hardest goal toward finding success is overcoming the daily fear of having to do things I don't always want to do. It is so easy to put things off in hope that whatever confrontation awaits me goes away somehow. Each and every issue should be dealt with one way or the other, but they must all be tackled regardless.

Each issue generally has one more individual's vested interest. I always try to find the best answer and then garnish it in an appetizing manner so that all stakeholders feel some satisfaction. That way they will want to deal with me again.

Bruce MacDonald
Senior Construction Manager, Facilities Development

Never underestimate the power of a team!

A pair, a trio, a quartet, a family, or a whole department … putting people together to solve problems usually results in the sum being greater than the parts.

The stories of famous artists and inventors that we hear most often are about creative individuals, and usually reinforce the notion that you have to be a creative genius for your ideas to be considered worthwhile. While it's true that individual "genius" often provides the spark for a great idea, at Imagineering putting people together in effective teams more often than not results in a series of sparks that turn into a bonfire.

In fact, over the years it has become clear that the most diverse teams—rather than the most homogenous groups—are often the most effective in seeing various aspects and multiple solutions to a need. When putting together a team, an astute team manager will sometimes deliberately "cast the talent" as well as personalities, in a way that encourages different points of view—and sometimes a certain degree of friction! This can be a tricky business, because a team who ultimately cannot agree or come to a decision can't be considered effective.

Part of that responsibility lies with the leader of the team—but leadership roles within a team can be flexible while still maintaining people's titles. It is often useful to have different people take the lead role on projects for several reasons: casting the lead role with "new talent" allows emerging leaders the opportunity to exercise their skills and augment their experience. It allows expression of new leadership styles and consequently new ideas on how to achieve goals. And it allows those who are typically used to being "the leader" to relax from that role for a while, and act as a mentor from the sidelines.

Because working with a team is the "norm" here, an emphasis is placed more on relationships and building respect within the group, rather than building up individual "stardom."

On my orientation day at Imagineering, I recall hearing a quote attributed to Marty Sklar which I remember still: "There is only one name on the door at Walt Disney Imagineering." Instead of measuring success by how many people recognized your talent "by name," a project is considered a success when all the puzzle pieces, assembled by many, many Imagineers, fit together in a cohesive way to serve the same stated purpose.

Anne Tryba
Manager, Graphic Design Department

91

Everyone who has passion for an idea can become very emotional. The passion can be about the ideas, the budget, the schedule. Let the conflict occur. Don't be afraid to participate in a passionate environment.

Don't shy away from conflict, it's an integral part of an evolution of an idea. Your idea must be able to withstand that conflict.

Take a breath before you react. Breathe, then respond.

Don't take the conflict personally. Make the distinction between you and your work. Fight for your work, but don't fight on a personal level.

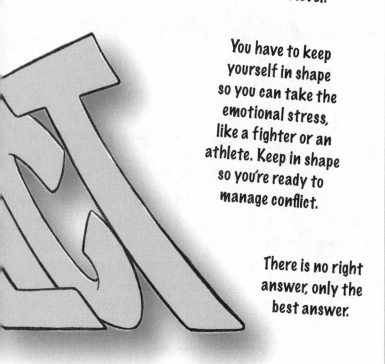

You have to keep yourself in shape so you can take the emotional stress, like a fighter or an athlete. Keep in shape so you're ready to manage conflict.

There is no right answer, only the best answer.

And don't forget the old emotional bank account—make sure you have enough deposits before you try to make a withdrawal.

The Value of Ideas, Part II

Idea and Instinct

It seems ideas come along in a "time stream"—I can't think of a better term.

I will be thinking along many lines and stop at elements to voice or evaluate, then go on thinking. In a group, that moves like waves. In an evolving project, it shows up as presented concepts, reviews, and so on. The concept round formalizes the ideas chosen.

We think of concepts as evolving toward getting better, but in complex projects the evolution carries with it a negative capital as well. When we go through a concept round, then another and another, it's often not clear why a concept is rejected or not embraced.

Many times a simplistic reason is abstracted, or no reason is given at all. We then look for more ideas to form a concept. When that next round starts, the field is not as fresh and clear as it should be. "We can't do this—it was in the last presentation" is often heard. Most of the secondary ideas, themes, and supporting elements are verboten. It's a typical case of throwing the baby out with the bathwater.

After three or four rounds, it becomes difficult to find ideas that everyone can get behind, and a lot of juicy secondary ideas are getting squeezed out by association. Before long, only general, safe, or generic ideas get through.

In fact, those biases can be there from the start: "I don't like this feature—it reminds me of the such-and-such at the 1933 World's Fair."

The first ideas that come out reflect more the instinctive, emotional, and intuitive response to a project. The later ideas tend to be more logical. Of course, it's not impossible to find the great thing after fifteen rounds, but I think it's rare.

Actually sometimes the process goes full circle, and one of the first ideas is reincarnated at a later time when people have mostly forgotten it.

My note to self: "Pay very close attention to the first three concepts that come out—they are usually the most fresh and unhindered. Core notions are likely worth going back to along the way. If nothing sticks after the third round, try changing the question or changing some of the people."

Paying close attention to the early instinctive ideas has another advantage: it can speed up the process. In fact, a lot of companies don't have the luxury of doing things multiple times and have to trust their instincts more.

Momentum in a project is very important—working on instinct also helps that a great deal, and people feel the energy of those ideas better.

It can be scary to take off with some of the early ideas, but we shouldn't be afraid of the prospect. Ultimately, what a project needs is not 200 random ideas—only a few very strong fundamental ones.

And they just might come up right away.

Luc Mayrand
Concept Designer

A Question of Time and Money

When is the design finished?

This often asked question has many answers. However, at Imagineering there are typically two that prevail: when we run out of time or when we run out of money.

The thing is that for a designer the job is really never finished. There is always room for improvement, and well there should be. We are never completely satisfied with our results, whether it's our first solution or the last.

We continually strive for perfection in design, which is ever elusive, but gets closer with each new iteration and with the more effort and energy that we apply. Nevertheless, even after an attraction or a shop or a hotel is finished and opened, the final product is always something that we feel we could improve on, if only we had more time or money!

So when *is* the design finished? Quite simply: never.

Orrin Shively
Executive Director, Research & Development

Thoughts and dreams ...
discipline and freedom ...
faith and fear ...
humor and strength ...
expression and discovery.
All the secrets to ...

Unharnessing Creativity

It Happens All the Time ...

You're driving down the freeway and suddenly realize that you've traveled several miles toward your destination, in perfect safety and comfort, and have absolutely no recollection of how you got there.

During those missing moments, you probably changed lanes a few times, sped up and slowed down with the traffic, maybe even transitioned onto a different freeway altogether. At least, your car did—because *you* certainly weren't driving it.

What happened is this: you've found one of the many on-ramps to the Imagineering Way.

Now, we don't mean that distracted semiconscious freeway driving is the key to creative thinking—we mean you've discovered an important skill that we all have inside us: the ability to lose reality without losing control. That's what Imagineering is all about. But do Imagineers really pile into their fancy company cars and set off down the freeway every time they need a new idea?

In a sense, yes. Everybody has two brains. Well, no, we don't really, no more than the big dinosaurs that science once thought had a spare brain in their tails. But for now, we'll just pretend we do. Your two brains occupy the exact same real estate in your cranium, but it turns out they're so different from each other that they might as well be at opposite ends of your body.

One brain is strict and regimented. It's like a marching band, or the Radio City Rockettes. The other brain is wild and spontaneous, like a jazz combo or the mosh pit at a headbangers' ball. One wears a top hat and tails; the other forgets to get dressed.

Here's the important part: one of those two brains is usually in charge, and that brain pretty much defines who other people think we are. And that bugs us.

One brain is what we are most of the time; the other is what we wish we could be. Whether we're naturally disciplined or naturally spontaneous, chances are we wish we could power up that other dormant brain. But how?

Whether your tendency is to line up with the Rockettes or leap into the mosh pit, all you have to do is find a way to keep the disciplined side of your brain busy.

That's why driving is such a petri dish of creativity. When you're driving a car, your disciplined brain is working overtime—keeping the car carefully centered between the white lines (a dream come true for that precision-oriented perfectionist), watching the speedometer, keeping the proper distance behind the car ahead, and once again plotting out that same old tried-and-true route you take every day.

And where is your undisciplined brain? It certainly isn't interested in driving, because there's nothing particularly creative about the process. (In fact, the Highway Patrol sternly frowns on any sort of spontaneous freeway improv.)

No, your undisciplined brain is down in the mosh pit, it's up in the clouds, out in space, dreaming and thinking, inventing and creating. It's free to be where it belongs.

So, your brains are happy, but where does that leave you? Well, unfortunately, you're out of the picture. You're a third entity in the equation—there are your two brains, and there's you. You're the fifth wheel, the chaperone tagging along on a date, the guest who doesn't know when to go home.

When you're driving a car—or rather, when your brain is driving a car—everything important is already taken care of. There's nothing much for you to do. Chances are, you're staring out the window, watching the scenery go by. Or you're sneaking a peek at the folks in the car next to you, or listening to the radio, or some other typically unproductive activity.

It would be best if you just got out of the way, and thought about something truly creative. Now's your chance!

You are not your brain. Your brains are like your arms or your fingers, your heart or your lungs. They do their best work when you stay out of their way. Just try listening to your heartbeat for a couple of minutes, or pay close attention to your breathing. Chances are, you'll get so worried about the whole process, you'll wind up hyperventilating.

Or try this when you're typing—figure out which finger presses the next key to spell out a word. You'll bring the whole typing process to an immediate standstill.

So, there you are: you try to help out, and you wind up hyperventilated and totally unproductive. The thing about creativity is this: don't think about it. And that's perfect, because that leaves the productive parts of your brain free to work.

Bruce Gordon
Project Director, Creative Development

Is There Discipline to Creativity?

There is a necessary struggle between discipline and looseness: take a jazz musician like Miles Davis, for example. His unstructured musical style succeeds because he had an enormous amount of discipline and training to back it up.

In any creative discipline, you must understand the process of any challenge you're undertaking, just like learning the scales of a musical instrument.

You also need to know the parameters of the game you're in, because no challenge is completely open ended. Establish what the expectations are. You need the built-in tension that thrives between wide-open thinking and a clearly defined set of expectations.

Creative people will often be more creative if they know the parameters—and on the flip side, not knowing the parameters can lead to frustration.

The Imagineers

Many people fear being fingered as the one who puts the crazy idea on the table, so they hold back. Sometimes the most bizarre-sounding solution turns out to be the simplest.

Don't self-edit—get a million ideas out on paper. There will be lots of people along the way who will edit for you, but they need to be able to choose from all the best ideas you can show them.

There are only 26 letters in the alphabet. How hard can writing be?

When facing a new challenge, let go of fear. There's nothing you can screw up that can't be fixed.

"And Then She Touched My Chicken ...

... and said, 'I already have everything I need.'"

That's the kind of conversation, overheard, that can get the creative juices bubbling merrily. What kind of chicken? Living? Cooked? Or, more sinister, a merely metaphorical bird? The reaction, so strong, so shocked. Was the woman touching the chicken in question a meddling mother-in-law, surly fast-food server, voodoo priestess?

Taking a bit of conversation and turning it into a little story is a great warm-up exercise for my craft: writing. I've learned that the best way to get going is just to do it, and, if I'm stuck, I can turn to these intriguing scenarios, crank out a few paragraphs, and return refreshed to my work. It's a little like improv, without an audience.

I happen to work best on deadline, but I still need to write every day. Inspiration for me is usually time-related, but sometimes I surprise myself. Certain tricks get fingers to keyboard or pen to paper and help remind me that I have a large fund of creativity that I can draw on when needed. I think a lot of creativity is simply self-confidence. You need to feel that you and your ideas are worthy of attention and respect. But to get them out is another thing.

A way to get the words flowing is to take a sentence from a book I'm reading and change a few key phrases. Harder is to take a striking passage and see if I can describe the same thing—a sudden rainstorm, an emotion—in a new way.

I also "warm up" sometimes without a plan ... by just writing whatever comes out and seeing where it takes me for about five minutes. I used to do it in cafés in college, and now I just sit in my office and let it flow. I don't correct my spelling or read back—I just keep at it for a few minutes. It is just like exercise. Or I take a word and riff on that—usually it's a word or concept I'm working on. When I get back to the assignment, whatever it is, I'm ready to go. It's like a little minivacation, and it lets things out—when I read back what I wrote—that I didn't know were there.

I think part of creativity is continually surprising yourself. Try something new—physical, social, intellectual—and you will approach it with a unique style. You'll both reaffirm your creativity and put it to use in a new field.

Mel Malmberg
Show Writer, Creative Development

Imagineers wear
many hats—
sometimes all
at once!

Scot Drake
Concept Designer,
Creative
Development

You encourage creativity
by assuring the people
around you that
"Your idea will be heard."

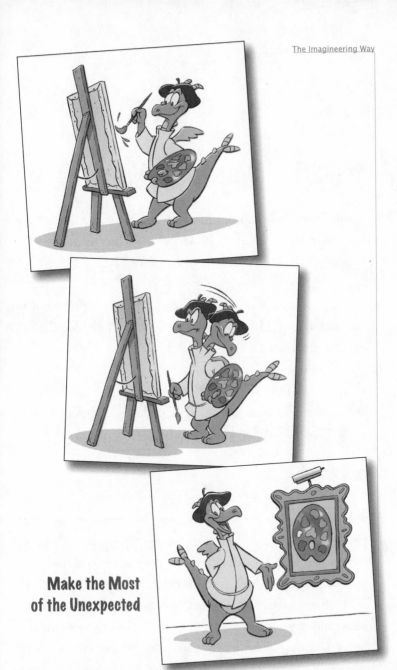

Make the Most of the Unexpected

Where Do You Get Your Ideas?

It was inevitable. Someone asked this to William Shakespeare when he wrote *Hamlet* … Pablo Picasso when he painted the *Guernica* … Eduard Haas when he invented PEZ.

And now somebody just asked me: "Where do you get your ideas?" The answer is usually something like, "Huh?" or "Oh … I dunno."

Well, I would like to answer the question by avoiding it and then answering a different question. I don't know "where," but I do know "how."

Here's How

There's an implication in the question "Where do you get your ideas?" that suggests that creative people know something we normal people do not. That, perhaps, there is a part of the brain, some accessory or high-speed Internet modem that "creative" people have, which allows them to connect to something special, something mysterious, something weird. And creative people, being naturally mischievous, cultivate this impression. Well, they're entitled, aren't they? Most aren't paid as well as doctors, stonemasons, nitro haulers, and other people who work for a living. It's a tough life, being creative nine to five.

It's taken me years to develop that faraway look in the eyes that implies the creative process is at work. Before I perfected it, I walked into a lot of lampposts and ladies' rest rooms (I am male). I had to learn that the unfocused gaze must be accompanied by a sharpening of the other senses. Ninjas do this, I suppose. And headwaiters.

Have you noticed, for instance, that here we are, quite a way down the page, and I haven't actually addressed my topic? Typical creative type at work. Think I'm rambling? Not on your life. This seemingly random, willy-nilly style is all part of the mysterious creative process—a process that anyone can enjoy.

The Creative Process

Let's say you've been assigned to come up with an idea. How do you go about it? First thing you do is freeze up. "I can't do that. I'm a foreman in a shoe factory. I can't just go off and think of something." Well cut that out. You've been terrorized by creative people. Don't let them get you down. The thugs! Not only is there nothing to it but you've been doing it all your life and calling it something else.

Let's say ... the TV remote is way over on the footstool, and you're on the couch with a plate of nachos balanced on your stomach. You have to be creative. Maybe you throw a shoe at the remote, trying to hit the channel button. Or you attempt a mind-control experiment to "will" the fireplace tools to tip over onto it. Or you ask the dog, "Fetch the remote—come on, Winston ... get it, get the remote! Want a nacho?" See? That's all creative thinking. The real problem, then, is when the official request comes down—to "think creatively"—you forget you've been doing it all your life.

How to Be Creative

There are two ways to be creative: 1) Listen to everyone. 2) Don't listen to anyone. Either way works. The point is, everything works if you expect it to. Take off your shoes. Wash your hair. Take a walk. Stay still. Keep moving. Talk. Stay silent. These techniques all work to initiate the creative process. Here are some others:

The magic 8-ball method. Grab your head and shake vigorously—then wait for an idea to float to the surface. Whatever comes into your head, say it out loud. If people laugh, they're probably just jealous.

Hang around creative people. This worked for Hemingway in Paris. It will work for you.

Hang around dull people. By comparison, you'll seem really clever. And you will eventually become so bored, your mind will shift into high gear. The ideas will just flow.

The process of elimination. Sometimes your best thoughts come to you in private. In the … you know. Be prepared to write your ideas down, wherever you are.

As a wise man once told me, "If you're going to be a success, you have to learn that simple, two-syllable word: 'dis-pline.'" Okay, so he wasn't exactly wise, and you don't really need discipline to be creative. But the point is, I remembered what he said. And whenever I need a laugh, I remember him. Sometimes a laugh is all you need to break the creative logjam.

You already know how to be creative. You just need "enthusiasm" (four syllables) and "faith" (one syllable). Get excited, then rely on your abilities. I firmly believe that the answer to any problem already exists. If you don't find it, it will find you. But don't listen to me. Are you listening? You're not? Good. Listen to yourself.

Michael Sprout
Senior Concept Writer, Creative Development

Unblocking the Creative Block

Walt Disney once said, "It's kind of fun to do the impossible." But sometimes when you burn out you think it's kind of impossible to do the fun!

You know you've done it before, but you start to wonder if you can do it again. You know you're only as good as your last idea. But once you realize it's okay to be uncomfortable and afraid, you won't be so afraid of being afraid.

Everyone knows there's a tremendous intimidation in just getting started. Sometimes you think you'd rather get a root canal or two than start on your project. So rather than getting started, think ahead, then reverse engineer it back to the solution. Look at the far end—imagine the experience you want people to have. Visualize the success of your idea. Then work your way backward to the solution until you find the obstacle.

Sleep on it, put it aside, and do something else. Wash the dishes, play tennis, go to the beach—and suddenly you'll find the block is gone, and you're ready to start.

The Imagineers

Countless sketches are created in our brainstorming sessions that are never presented to anyone—case in point, this exploration of alternatives to "Shark Reef" at Typhoon Lagoon. We ended up designing a great water park because we always allow ourselves to have fun.

SHARK BRIEF

Kathy Mangum
Vice President, Creative Development

I like to employ something I call *The Goldilocks Principle:* allow yourself to think up three solutions before you proceed with any single one. Like Goldilocks, with three choices, you allow yourself to have one that's too big, one that's too small, and one that's just right. You can then proceed with the confidence that the solution you choose to pursue is the best solution.

Bruce Vaughn

The Facts of Fantasy

Any time I am in need of an idea, I will look to facts first. Facts are the best foundation for creating fantasies—the imagination anchors best in what we know. Once anchored, it allows us to spin and weave threads of information into an idea.

I like to pick the facts that are the most exciting to me and then check them out to see if they interest others. When others respond to facts that are recognizable, it is easier to engage them in ideas that have a familiar ring before taking them off unexpectedly into the world of fantasy.

Once I have a concept in mind, I think about the best way to express it through design—the language of color, line, rhythm, shape, and form. My favorite place to see the language of design at work is in a garden. Nature has a limitless budget and no preconceived notions as to what a design should be.

Of course, the best part of having an idea and designing it is producing it. Building it is a test of my foresight (how well I planned) as well as the ultimate test of my ability to be flexible when the inevitable changes occur.

Peggy Van Pelt
Imagineer

Creativity ...
It's about the journey,
as much as it is about the destination.

To be creative is to be curious, and to be curious involves risk. So, to accept the challenge of creativity, one must be ready to embark on an unpredictable emotional, cognitive, and sometimes even physically challenging journey.

To scale a mountain is nothing in comparison to assaulting a blank piece of paper or raw canvas. To create something out of nothing is the ultimate challenge—and the ultimate opportunity. To create an idea is only the first part of the journey. To create a reality built from the dream is the greater part of the journey.

To pursue a creative vision or aspiration alone is filled with many rewards. To participate in the process of Disney Imagineering is the ultimate in fulfillment. The Disney creative process harnesses the power and potential of a "team" to a vision.

Once a creative vision has been established, like a distant summit viewed by a climber before the ascent, it becomes the mission of the Disney team to carefully steward an original idea toward its final reality. As the team progresses with its "climb," the summit's view may occasionally be obscured or lost through trees and rock outcroppings. There may even be a need to change the approach to the ascent as obstacles change the perspective and pose unforeseen challenges on how to best reach the "summit." Never losing the essence of the original idea is the challenge as the journey progresses.

Reaching the destination, a reality created from a dream, is like reaching one of the world's most challenging summits. There is a real sense of accomplishment and satisfaction on the part of the entire team owing to the success of the "climb," and the view is spectacular!

Equally special is the fact that the view usually reveals the challenge of yet another unclimbed peak, an opportunity to plunge once more into a unique journey led by creativity.

Rick Rothschild

Executive Show Director, Senior Vice President
Creative Development

Visualize the Space

One of the challenges of Imagineering—or any design project—involves creating a certain concept of space. Visualize the space as an actual image, a two-dimensional "rough" on a surface, such as a pencil line on white paper. Scale can be assigned by adding a person to the drawing.

Now, visualize some of the important detail to the drawing, and add relative space and form. Along with all of this visualizing, note the changing colors. Now, other people can understand your concept and add to it or share it.

If the concept includes a mechanical or physical element, such as a ride experience for a Disney Park, one must sometimes talk to an engineer to establish limitations or possibilities. Also, consulting with a musician to support the feeling if the imagined mood is a necessary part of the concept.

And for everyday routine problems, I think the ability to visualize certain changes might make realization possible for anyone to improve his or her daily life.

John Hench
Senior Vice President, Creative Development

The process of Imagineering is very simple: Creative creates an idea. Support team members develop the idea into reality. Millions of guests enjoy the idea.

What's key in Imagineering is the PASSION with which the Creative and Support team members work together to develop the idea into a Disney product, the finest family entertainment product in the world.

Chalmer Day
Program Manager, Project Coordination

My first rule is what I call my MICKEY RULE:

"Manage It Correctly —
Keep Everything Yippee"

The word "yippee" in the dictionary is defined as "interjection expressing delight or excitement." (I know it sounds corny, but it works!)

Barry Golding
Principal Technician, Electrical Production

Most "new innovations" are not new at all. They are simply clever applications of tried-and-true technologies.

When faced with a complex problem, look for the simplest solution.

We are surrounded by technology and science which we see as valuable resources, but we sometimes forget that common sense is often our most valuable asset.

John M. Polk
Principal Special Effects Designer

If you have five minutes to do a project, spend four minutes figuring out how to do it and one minute doing it.

Walk, Talk, Calm

The time has come for me to write,
But all my brain cells seem uptight.
I think my writing neurons shrank.
The page before me just stays blank.

The diagnosis? "Writer's block."
Ideas stuck in thought gridlock.
But I have ways to break the jam,
Each a proven battering ram.

One great technique is just GET OUT!
I ambulate and move about.
This feeds my head more oxygen,
And inspiration rocks again.

Another way incorporates,
A tête-à-tête with my teammates.
Our deepest thoughts or idle chatter
Always sparks my ol' gray matter.

I might also find a quiet place,
And meditate on empty space.
Once I relax all through and through,
EUREKAs pop out of the blue.

So, when nasty blocks clog my head,
I don't react with fear or dread.
I see them as a needed test
That forces me to do my best.

And with these ways I will succeed—
Walk, Talk, Calm are guaranteed.
Like trusted friends
    I've come to know 'em.
Why … they helped me write
    this here poem.

Scott Hennesy

Show Writer/Show Adaptation Specialist, Creative Development

Crastination:
A Job Best Left to the Pros

There's a fine line between "professional" and "amateur," especially when someone loves what he or she is doing. One thing's for sure, though—we Imagineers are all pros.

And there's one area where that's truer than ever—the subject of "crastination." Boy, are we pros at that. You'd be hard-pressed to find more pro crastinators than we have at Imagineering. We are world-class, indeed.

There's an unpopular saying that goes, "The best work is that which is done at the last minute." Unpopular, that is, among bosses, teachers, and parents. While that saying may fly in the face of everything we've been taught since we were kids, there are those who just happen to believe it's true.

How so? Well, let's look at another tried-but-true aphorism: "Success is ninety-nine percent perspiration and one percent inspiration." Very true, of course, but here's what they don't want you to realize: inspiration is ninety-nine percent desperation. As in, "My report is due tomorrow, and I haven't started it yet."

Crastination, when properly performed by a pro, is nothing to be ashamed of. You see, the mind is like an engine that spends most of its day in "idle," coasting along as you go about your normal daily routine. Face it, most of our jobs, schools, and daily tasks don't really tax our brains all that much.

Do you really think you're going to sit down and write a brilliant report with your mind's engine in its normal semi-stalled state? No, if you really want to be a pro, if you're hoping to downshift the gears and kick the accelerator, your mind needs some sort of serious stimulus. And what better stimulus than the high-grade panic of true desperation? Ah, desperation—rocket fuel for a sedentary mind!

Now, you might think that waiting until the last minute is a very risky approach. What if inspiration doesn't strike? Well, believe me, not taking the last-minute approach has some dangerous pitfalls of its own. For example, ideas that come along too soon, when there's still plenty of time before the deadline, are at risk of being overthought. We all know that overthinking is one of the great bugaboos of creativity. Overthink can ruin any idea, especially a good one. But if the idea isn't discovered until moments before the deadline, there's no time to over think it. The idea is safe.

Coming up with an idea way ahead of the deadline also carries with it the risk of making your job look too easy. If you've finished the school assignment or work report way too early, you obviously didn't take it seriously … you didn't try very hard … or your teacher or boss isn't giving you enough to do. Coming up with a brilliant idea at the very last minute—rocket fueled by that overwhelming sense of desperation—can make you look like a true miracle worker.

In contrast, there are definite pluses to waiting until desperation strikes. For example, think of all the other stuff you can get done while you're crastinating, like finishing up your *previous* assignment, which has now reached *its* last-minute state!

Now I'm not recommending that we put aside our work and spend our days doing things that are definitely more interesting and appealing than the unavoidable assignment. We don't want everyone going back to work or school, saying the Imagineers said it was okay to leave it all to the last minute.

After all, crastination is a job best left to the pros. Especially the ones with their tongues planted firmly in their cheeks.

Bruce Gordon
Imagineer and Professional Crastinator

Procrastination: The Writer's Curse

At Imagineering we always start with a blank piece of paper, which can be very exciting or very scary, depending on your mood that day.

Writers are natural procrastinators as it is, so I've found that the best way to approach anything is to make sure that piece of paper stays blank for as short a time as possible.

Get something on it, even if you know it's not right. At least you will have gotten started.

Walt always said, "The way to get started is to stop talking and start doing." That's true in our work and it's true in life. Stop talking about all your dreams and do something. Get something on paper. Get started.

You may not get it right, but at least you'll have it in writing.

Jason Surrell
Show Writer, Creative Development

Creative Stuff from Boring Numbers

In my role as a project estimator, it is common to see people viewing cost constraints as a primary part of the challenge Imagineers must solve. What I think some miss is how cost limits can themselves be instrumental in producing creative solutions.

This can be as simple as making the blank sheet of paper a known size so the blue sky ideas can flow. It can be the knowledge that a previous design can't be reused, so new and fresh ideas must be produced.

I've seen cost constraints motivate the team to produce a solution that looks better and lasts longer than the "real thing"—the status quo choice if costs weren't being considered.

Not earthshaking, but who else might say this if not an estimator?

Jeff McCain

Principal Project Estimator, Project Estimating

Pithy Quotes and Thoughtful Insights:

Every design job takes at least two people: the designer and somebody to break the designer's pencil.

It is better to have a clear vision and a sound plan, and accept the possibility of failure, than to have neither and remove all doubt.

Change happens.

The only thing standing between one big creative idea and success is about a million small creative solutions.

Sometimes the best way to come up with something interesting is to combine two or more good ideas. This is not the same as a hybrid, which usually results from the combination of lousy ideas.

Generalists are more likely to discover creative solutions than specialists.

Any day you learn something useful is a good day.

Discovery is the flip side of creativity.

Bill Willcox
Principal Engineer, Ride Mechanical Systems

Fear of Creativity and the Redeeming Quality of Humor

Walt Disney wondered "if 'common sense' isn't another way of saying 'fear,' and 'fear' too often spells failure." It seems to me that the fear of trying something new is the fear of the discomfort that comes when one is forced to redefine oneself.

When you create, you are essentially—even in a small way—reinventing who you are and what you believe yourself capable of accomplishing. There is a kind of courage that has to be mustered before embarking on any creative endeavor, no matter how large or small.

It seems that "practicing creativity" is like exercising a set of muscles. The more you take creative chances, the easier it is to see whether your idea will succeed or fall by the wayside. You take that deep breath and go. And by looking back at the small chances taken, it becomes clearer that bigger risks can be "survived."

Creativity requires a great deal of experimentation, and many mistakes. What the public doesn't see, when the completed successful idea is out there, is the huge pile of "almost-hits-but-mostly-misses" on the way to the final success story.

Sometimes, too, individual designers are so intimately involved with an idea that they lose perspective on what is good about it, and what could use improvement. When I was part of a team of designers assigned to develop the logo for Disney's Animal Kingdom, we wrestled with the challenge of how to express a whole theme park in a recognizable symbol. After a few days, we came together to review our ideas. I had been working hard to incorporate symbols for the two main park themes—real animals and fantasy animals—into a detailed silhouette for the huge "Tree of Life" icon that dominates the park. I did several variations, proud of the way it all fit together like a neat little puzzle. It wasn't until I had put it up on the wall with the others that I realized it looked like the silhouette of Bozo the Clown!

Without the ability to laugh at one's errors, and at oneself, it is hard to allow others the luxury of making mistakes. A sense of humor is one of the most important tools we have when it comes to maintaining an atmosphere of creativity. This sense of lightness and humor as a "company culture" comes from "the top down," and is recognized as a way of fostering a safe haven within our campus. Imagineering works hard to keep humor reverberating through its halls.

Anne Tryba
Manager, Graphic Design Department

Get Lost!
Literally and figuratively.

I've made some of my greatest discoveries while lost. Getting lost is frustrating, but it's also one of the most important things that can happen to you. At worst, information and learning come out of getting lost; at best: wonderful, serendipitous, and sometimes profitable discoveries can take place.

On your journeys take a map along, look at it, memorize some of it, then put it in your back pocket and don't take it out until you *really* need it. Maps are a starting point and life preserver. The getting-lost part in the middle is where the good stuff happens.

And even if you're not lost, change direction once in a while—do something uncomfortable ...

Change your path in the supermarket, take a different route to work, tune in to a new radio station, listen to a commentator that you don't agree with, wear something "not your style," eat something new, buy different stuff at the store, read a book or magazine backward. If you like cool climates, try warm. If you like Italy, go to Iceland. Get out of your ruts—it will really expand your way of thinking, how you see things, how people see you, and what your overall perceptions are.

Objects in the mirror are not what they appear … and people, places, and things are not always what they seem.

The seductive lobby often leads to an ugly hotel. The shabby alley may hide an incredible restaurant. Take an interesting "dead end" street—it may actually lead to a network of avenues, not really be a dead end. Go into an unattractive or cluttered shop or junk store—there may be a treasure in there.

Life is a trip and an education. Don't be afraid of the stop signs, dangerous curves, and bumps in the road.

Tom Morris
Vice President, Executive Producer, Creative Development

Creativity can be so hard, it can hurt.
When you're in the middle of a creative block,
you're ready to strangle everyone around you.
"There's no other solution," you want to yell.
"I've given you every one there is."
Soon you even start to think, I don't belong
here anymore—I can't do this anymore.

David Durham
Director, Concept Integration, Creative Development

Thinking inside
the box ... thinking
outside the box.

Chris Turner
Concept Designer
Creative Development

You've Got to Bait the Hook ...

... and an irresistible story is the temptation that reels your audience in. Storytelling is the best way to sell any idea in any sort of situation.

But remember to keep the story simple—think of it as balancing a complex idea on the head of a pin. When you get it right, it becomes an implosion of concepts—your idea synthesized into a clean, simple statement of a few words. Try to brush it on with a feather stroke, rather than laying it on with a trowel. And don't cloud it all up with too many details!

Compliment your audience's intelligence by leading them to understand. Make them reach for it, though, and you'll find they do so instinctively. Make them say, "Look what I did!"

There's one more ingredient to selling your idea—make sure you're always part of the team. Take a "group bow" with everyone else who contributed to the final product. We all nurture and inspire each other, and the greatest delight is discovering that joy of cooperation between creative minds.

Richard M. Sherman
Songwriter and Composer, Honorary Imagineer

Designing Interactive Worlds

Marshall McLuan once said that those who distinguish between entertainment and education don't know much about either. We don't learn math in a movie. But we do learn a ton about human nature, which is necessary if we are to live happy, successful lives. Understanding that learning is a major part of art also helps explain the difference between stories and games.

Watching stories we learn by example. Playing games we learn by experience. This difference focuses itself around who controls the protagonist. In a story it's the storyteller. In a game it's the player. And it's this feature that trips up so many "creatives." Most of us are trained in storytelling, not game-making. In an attempt to control the flow of the game we often resort to storytelling techniques that inadvertently remove control of the protagonist from the player, leaving the player confused about his or her role in the game and frustrated. (It's also why all the "interactive stories" seem to fail except as novelties.)

So the first rule of thumb in designing games is "never take control away from the player." If you look at good games you'll see that the rule is always obeyed. Once the game has started the player remains in control until the game is over. The only exception is in some games where control is removed at the ends of "chapters," natural breaking points in the flow of the action, like the end of an inning in baseball or a level in a computer game.

The second rule applies to the design process—"Let the guest be your guide." Forget the "director as dictator with a vision" Hollywood moviemaking stuff. Though you do need a vision (guests aren't game designers) you can't dictate to them how they're going to read your design. They are going to act based upon their interpretation of what you've laid out. And you will be constantly surprised at how they misinterpret your design intent. You generally want to only sketch the outline of the game and let the guests fill in the details on their own. Rather than telling a specific story, here you build a general world and let the guest fill in the specifics of their own story as they play. And you'll discover that unlike a story, the more flexible your world is, the more ways in which it can be interpreted, the stronger the game will be.

The third rule is "design through mock-ups and play tests." Each medium has its own, specialized shorthand used to outline and develop a concept during its design. Films use storyboards. Rides use models. Games use mock-ups. Try to imagine trying to sell Tetris or PacMan with only a storyboard or model. Without the animation and interactivity there's no magic. That lies in the play, in the behavior that the guest gets lured into. Mock-ups and play tests also are the only way to confirm that the world you're inventing is truly an intriguing place to play in. And, it's the tool to use to work through the myriad of blind alleys, areas of confusion and so forth that every game must rid itself of before the design is complete.

Finally remember that though it's not always true, stories tend to be proportionally more literal while games are more symbolic. Stories focus on human-scale interactions and teach about personal level things while games tend to focus more on structural aspects of the culture. Chess is about military strategy. Monopoly is about buying and selling. Baseball and computer games teach us the value of hard work, that there is honor in failure and that if you keep trying eventually you will win. And all of these are heavily symbolic. Football teaches us about territoriality. Primates mark territory with feces. We are primates. It is no coincidence that a play in football starts when a dung-shaped ball is passed between the legs of a player and that it's the position of that dung upon the field that determines what territory belongs to whom.

 **Joe Garlington**

Executive Director–Senior Show Producer, Creative Development

Shut down for a while. There's a rhythm to your soul—you generate and regenerate. Read a poem, listen to a song, go see a play. Feed your creative self. Sometimes it doesn't make sense on a balance sheet, but its importance and value are unquantifiable.

Take someone new on a tour of what you've done to get yourself inspired about what you do. Show others what you do to reinvigorate yourself.

When I was eating dinner one day I had two napkins in front of me. I grabbed one napkin to scribble down an especially pithy thought. I saved the napkin, filed it away, and still have it today.

I grabbed the other napkin to wipe the barbecue sauce off my chin, crumpled it up, and threw it away.

Which napkin will you be?

Chopping Up Creative Challenges

It's amazing what you can learn from the most trivial things— like chopping wood, for instance. When my dad first taught me to chop wood, I don't think he realized it would teach me some of the most valuable lessons I've learned about overcoming creative challenges—crafting a game plan, putting in 100 percent effort, utilizing additional resources, taking a new point of view, wearing a lot of plaid flannel. The lessons I learned chopping hundreds of logs into smaller logs are ones that I still use today when faced with creative challenges.

An unsplit log, like a creative challenge, just sits there, waiting for you to do something. It's necessary to have a game plan, and obviously, an ax to get the job done (leather gloves don't hurt, either). Are you gonna chop little pieces off the edges until the log is gone, are you gonna hit this side or that side, or are you just gonna whack it right down the middle? You can think about how to do it all you want, but don't think too much. Because in the end, the only way to split the log and solve the challenge is to hit it … and hit it hard.

A halfhearted effort will achieve nothing—except maybe getting your ax stuck in the log. Jump in feet first and crack it as hard as you can. After one or two tries, the log splits in two. The challenge is solved, and it's on to the next one.

Of course, it's not always that easy—sometimes no matter how hard you try, the log won't split. Maybe there's a knot in the log or the wood is too green. Sometimes you need some more help to get the job done. You may have to ask for advice from another person, get more information, try a new tactic.

Sometimes what it takes to solve a challenge is to look at it from another angle, a different view, a new perspective. Turn your thinking—I mean, that log—upside down and start chopping at it from the bottom. Who knows—maybe the whole thing will open up … or maybe it won't. Thirty minutes of hand-numbing wood chopping, and you've still got one now very annoying log staring you right in the sweaty face.

And that's when the most overlooked and easiest solutions can present themselves from out of nowhere. That's when your father hands you the chain saw. "Why didn't you give me this before?" I ask. To which he replies, "I didn't know you were going to need it until now." There you have it— mission accomplished.

Jason Grandt

Graphic Designer, Architecture and Engineering

The creative climate changes like the weather ...

Working your way through a challenge is like riding a rowboat in a storm. Everyone in the boat knows how to row, but when a storm comes up, the waves and wind can hit you from any direction. To make it through the storm, you have to keep rowing in the right direction while giving the boat the freedom to go left and right as it needs to. And remember, your team members are your rudders.

I find it helpful, when mired in day-to-day politics and problems, to pick my head up, look over the fray, and focus on the end user of my project—the park guest. I picture the guests having a more enjoyable day, or perhaps being safer, or receiving a greater "wow" factor, because of my work. Such refocusing off the problems and on to the benefits of what I'm doing seems to instantly motivate me to put my head back down and tackle the problems.

Bill West
Senior Software Engineer, Scientific Systems
Show/Ride Engineering

Naysayers and Affirmation

Ultimately, the security of affirmation has to come from within. But to get started, you need some affirmation from the outside. However, if you rely only on affirmation from others, you will find yourself starting to listen to the naysayers and you will eventually fail.

When you're five years old and singing your heart out in front of family and friends, everyone applauds, even though you were awful. But that early affirmation gives you the strength to continue until you finally learn to be good.

Eventually, you will become strong enough so that much of your affirmation can come from within.

Most naysayers aren't malicious. They are the ones who need the affirmation. You must change your perception of naysayers—think of them as having aesthetic pneumonia. Help them change. Come to the table with a little bit of aesthetic penicillin. And remember, it's your responsibility to keep them from draining you!

The Imagineers

Creativity and Choice

Choice is a basic function of being human: we choose what we wear and watch; we choose to supersize that meal (or not); we choose to listen, or sing, how to arrange the fridge, whether to squash a spider or let it live. It's moral, aesthetic, organizational, nutritional.

Decisions come from somewhere, from something we bring to the editing table: memory, allusion, aversion, emotion. It's good to acknowledge where our often mysterious responses come from, what pathways we take to a solution, so that the game of choice can be played endlessly from a root source.

I have a spot in my garden that gets a lot of sun and plenty of water. I like roses because of the movie Citizen Kane and the sled Rosebud. And I'm planting this rosebush because I like the color—blush—of this particular flower. It doesn't hurt that it's named "Orson."

I have a spot in my garden that gets a lot of sun and plenty of water. I like roses because the scent reminds me of my grandmother. I'm planting this rosebush because I want lots of sweet-smelling flowers and it grows to four feet high, just the height of my brick fence.

I have a spot in my garden that gets a lot of sun and plenty of water. I like roses, not as much as rhododendrons, but the rhodies need shade and coolness and I've learned the hard way—the reason that spot is empty is that I had a rhododendron there and it died. So I guess I'll go with roses, this white one that has lots of little blooms and looks a bit like a rhododendron if you squint.

I have a spot in my garden that gets a lot of sun and plenty of water. I hate all flowers so I'm putting a boulder there. But it has to be a nice, smooth boulder so that I can sit on it, sending bad vibes to flowers everywhere. I'm concentrating on the ones in the rest of my yard first.

So choice can engender a lot of responses to one simple starting point.

That's creativity in a nutshell—responses. But the responses have to be right for the job—at least in someone's opinion. It might as well be your opinion—it's your garden—so exercise it, make the choice, and move on.

At Imagineering, you're never working in a vacuum, even if you're working alone. Around the corner is a colleague or a meeting, and your idea will be put to the test. The end product doesn't have to be transparent if the solution is right, but you'd better be able to defend it—to justify your choices. Then there's consensus building, and group choices large and small.

Choice implies both freedom—an environment that encourage choosing—and abundance—something to choose from. At Imagineering, we have both: a lot of ideas constantly brewing and the freedom to glom onto one (or many) and ride them for all they are worth.

Often in a project's development, ideas fly thick and fast and it seems there are too many choices—everything looks good. Sometimes ideas compete and teams coalesce around a couple of ideas.

At the end of the competition, there may be a clear standout for the best option, but chances are the two ideas will each have merits that enhance the other. By guiding the other team through your logic, your pathway of choices, they can glean ideas for their own project.

Having the courage to choose is essential. When Walt Disney died, the company decided to go ahead with

Epcot, his idea for the Experimental Prototype Community of Tomorrow, though they didn't really know what it would be. When two models of competing ideas were pushed together, the combo was "it"—and management had the courage to say this is the answer, let's build it.

Of course, you can choose not to choose, to go back to the beginning and start over again. That takes real courage, since it costs big bucks to throw everything away and start again from scratch. Walt was well known for doing this in both films and theme park attractions—Pirates of the Caribbean was well underway as a walk-through when the idea for the boat ride surfaced. Construction was stopped, designs were revised, and, through the courage to start over, one of the greatest theme park attractions of all time was born.

And of course, the ultimate choice is to ignore all this wisdom we're offering, and go forward on your own!

Mel Malmberg
Show Writer, Creative Development

Making that dream come true ...
Changing perceptions ...
succeeding and failing ...
juggling deadlines and facing challenges ...
all while keeping ...

A Thousand Balls
in the Air

If people knew how hard I work to get my mastery,
it wouldn't seem so wonderful at all.

—Michelangelo

Perceptions of Success

I always scribbled and doodled, from the very beginning. My mom, who dabbled in watercolors, gave me my first set of paints when I was only three. I never considered myself an artist, as I was always making gifts for others, as all children do.

My mom told a story in later years about an airy line drawing of mine with a bold dash of blue under a magnificent swirl of pink. She would recall that I presented it proudly. "What is it, dear heart?" she asked as she turned it around and around.

I stuck my four-year-old chin out and with all the indignation of a misunderstood genius, turned it the proper way and retorted, "It's an elephant getting out of the bathtub!" Soon it was framed, matted, under glass, and hung with pride in the hall, for all to see. My self-belief was started.

Winning and mastery are something that we all wrestle with at some point in our lives. It is a process—the ballet bar exercises, if you will, that we all eventually learn—that gets us better. Most folks who work out will tell you "no pain … no gain." The same goes for psychological, emotional muscle—the stuff character comes from.

I had an experience about twenty years ago, which forever changed my feelings about excellence and what it means to succeed. I was still new to Southern California, I had no family here, and friends were not lifelong yet. I was thrilled to be working at Imagineering, but I was lonely and felt unconnected and adrift. I saw a call in a newspaper for volunteers for the Special Olympics at the Los Angeles Coliseum, so off I went.

They put me to work, and I found my main job was to monitor this one young lady in the 100-Yard Dash. Like many of the folks who competed that day, "Penny" was a Down's syndrome kid—about twelve years of actual age, and somewhat delightfully younger in reality. And that is exactly what I was to learn from her—all about reality.

There were five girls in the race. They were nervous. They each had an adult, like myself, individually assigned to them, to get them in the starting blocks and to calm them while waiting for the starting pistol. There were probably 3,000 to 4,000 people—family and fans—in the stands.

The guy shooting the starter's pistol was Southern California's answer to breathtaking beauty. Model material, this guy had a smile and a voice that would soothe a frightened tiger. The girls were mesmerized. Concentration was difficult, even for those of us who only qualified for Ordinary, not Special.

There were several false starts. Nerves were high. Finally "Beautiful Bob" had all five runners relaxed and we had a clean start with a bang on "go." The girls took off running, but after about twenty-five yards my little one stopped in the middle of the track and got down in the starting position again!

Meanwhile, the crowd is cheering and roaring. I run onto the track and start yelling, "Run … Go!" She's stagnant, planted firmly, crouched in the start position. The other runners have all crossed the finish line. Now the crowd sees my girl and starts yelling, "Go … go … go!" Beautiful Bob sees this and throws me a questioning look. I run out to my girl and say, "Sweetheart, run." She looks at me with her biggest smile and says, "After the gun goes bang!"

I speed back to Beautiful Bob and yell, "Shoot the gun! Shoot the gun again!" As I hurry back to my eager young athlete, I see Bob run to the infield up alongside her. We all three yell, "Ready, set, go!" Bob shoots the starter pistol and she's off again—and after another twenty-five yards she's down again. So now, finally, we get it.

Bob and I get abreast of her again. The crowd is chanting, "Go … go … go …" We holler, "Ready, set, go!" With another bang of the starter pistol, off she goes, and after about twenty yards she's down again. By now, everyone in the stadium has got her game. Bob motions me to take the pistol on the infield. He runs to the finish line, gets another huge ribbon strung across—and he kneels on the track dead center, arms open wide—his huge smile just for her. I raise the pistol.

The crowd now yells in unison, "Ready … set … go!" I shoot on "go" and she's off, hurtling herself as fast as she has ever gone—through the ribbon to a screaming crowd. Bob catches her on the other side and throws her skyward. I will forever remember her grin—open and wide with exultation, her face to the heavens above, yelling, "I WON!"

There was not a dry eye anywhere in that Coliseum. For she spoke absolute truth, and there was not one person out of those 4,000 fans who would have argued the point.

Talk about power. She single-handedly changed everyone's perception—to her own—without malice, force, or any hint of "victimhood." What everyone would have previously perceived as failure was now perceived as success, simply because my beautiful young athlete could see it no other way. That's true mastery in my mind.

Karen Connolly Armitage
Senior Concept Designer, Creative Development

"Good enough"
is the enemy of
anything great.

Chris Runco
Senior Concept Designer
Creative Development

Take the path less traveled,
knowing full well you're going to get
into trouble for doing it.

I submit to you that in the formula
world we live in, it's the people with
imagination—the risk takers—who
make the new waves and the new rules.
Remember, the last three letters of
trend are e-n-d.

Marty Sklar

Imagineers—Ready and Willin'

For me, the vision—the idea—it emerges on its own, whether I am asleep or engaged in completely different interests.

The creative image comes, it will come, it does come, and Imagineers must be receptive to record the idea in word or sketch. Survival of the vision depends on nourishment by the will, and without the Imagineers' being willin' …

… Willin' to fight for the creative image

… Willin' to believe in not giving up

… Willin' to protect the tools

… Willin' to become the Guardian of Creativity against the battles, the all-out war and tension between creative exhilaration and marketplace challenges

… Willin' to evaluate and be evaluated

… Willin' to push the boundaries and barriers again and again

… Willin' to go down and willin' to be lifted up

… Willin' to strive for improvement and excellence beyond "just good enough"

… Without Imagineers who are Ready and Willin'

… There is no Imagineering.

Paul Comstock
Director of Landscape Design

Gettin' the Gotchas

Someone connected with film animation once observed that there are only two phases to any project: "too early to tell" and "too late to do anything about it." This notion has always struck me as having profound relevance to the creative process at Imagineering.

A major challenge for any design team is to gain as much confidence as possible in the ultimate success of their idea as early as possible in the design process. To do this, the design team employs a variety of tools ranging from written story lines to sketches, renderings, models, and even computer simulations to help themselves and others to "previsualize" their idea. The trick is to come as close as possible to actually experiencing the attraction before it literally is too late to address the problems.

Because our projects are so complex and require the collaboration of so many different disciplines, it is a major challenge to ferret out the potential "gotchas" early in the design process. We have another saying at Imagineering about "not knowing what you don't know." This is code for the idea that it takes time, money, and the dedicated efforts of a variety of different types of talent to get to the point where the team is even able to ask the right questions. The "previsualization" tools are invaluable in enabling all of the different disciplines to bring their knowledge and creativity to the idea in an effective and constructive way. In other words, an important key to successful collaborative design is to be sure that everyone is working on the same idea.

Another key is trust. A successful design team has to foster an atmosphere where everyone is not only comfortable asking difficult questions but where team members are rewarded for challenging assumptions and forcing "skeletons out of closets." No matter how seductive an idea may be on its surface, if it contains flaws that will compromise its creative intent, a strong design team wants to identify the problems sooner rather than later.

Problems identified during the "too early to tell" phase of design have a good chance of being solved without causing irreparable damage to the core idea. Problems identified in the "too late to do anything about it" phase of the project are either impossible to address or impossibly expensive to fix.

Either way, the design team and, ultimately, the audience loses.

Barry Braverman
Vice President, Creative Development

Sometimes the Answer Is Right in Front of You

Several months before the opening of Epcot, the Show Lighting team fired up the eighty-four exterior lights on the monumental sphere of Spaceship Earth—and it was immediately obvious that the strong white light flattened the texture and cancelled out the facets on the sphere. The solution was to introduce color. But what color should it be?

For several days we had been treated to some spectacular Florida sunsets, the kind that make one stop and notice. The satin aluminum facets of Spaceship Earth reflected the color of these breathtaking sunsets. I realized I couldn't possibly do better than the colors that I was being shown by nature. So I inverted the sunset—yellow at the bottom, blending up to gold, then to lavender and pale blue, and finally into the deepest of blues of the night sky.

The design turned out to be an atmospheric mantel of color wrapped around the geometric solid sphere—a sunset that lasts the entire night for the guests at Epcot, an answer that had been right in front of me every evening.

Joe Falzetta
Principal Show Lighting Designer, Show Lighting

Nothing should be easy. If you don't fail some of the time, then you're not pushing hard enough. And those failures are usually the best learning tools.

Jack Gillett, Principal Imaging and Effects Designer
Imaging & Effects

Three maxims:

• Talk to the experts, but listen to everyone— they might be knowledgeable in the subject you're seeking.

• *Saru mo ki kara ochiru*—a Japanese phrase meaning, "Even monkeys sometimes fall from trees." We all make mistakes, we should learn from them, but not dwell on them.

• No show is better than a bad show.

Chris Bodden
Senior Special Effects Designer
Imaging & Effects

Forward Thinking
and Backward Perceptions

For the climactic scene in the Indiana Jones Adventure at Disneyland, we wanted the ride vehicle to suddenly start backing up as the giant rolling boulder comes thundering toward us.

Having a ride vehicle back up in the middle of a ride is something that's never been done, because it's not possible—with eighteen vehicles traveling down the track at the same time, a vehicle going in reverse would collide with the next vehicle coming toward it along the track. But if you've ever ridden the Indiana Jones attraction, you know your vehicle *does* suddenly start backing up. Or at least, that's your perception.

Your vehicle has actually stopped. It's the walls and ceiling that are moving, giving you the undeniable feeling that you're traveling backward. All through your life, your mind has been taught that small things move and big things don't— therefore, it must be your vehicle that is moving, not the entire cave! Perception is a learned thing, but it can often be wrong.

So where did we come up with this very effective solution? Well, we've learned to look for inspiration in the real world, because that's where the best solutions usually are. And what's the real-world equivalent of our Indiana Jones scene?

A car wash. One of those self-service machines at the gas station where you pull your car in and park while a series of brushes and spray heads mounted above and beside your car slowly travel back and forth. As I was sitting in my car one time, waiting for the car wash to begin, I found myself suddenly pressing on the brake pedal, thinking my car was rolling backward. But no, the gearshift was in park. It was the cleaning machine that had begun to move. The perception of my car being in motion was totally convincing, even when I knew the reality.

Sometimes when you see the answer to a perplexing challenge, it doesn't register in your mind because it's framed in such a completely different context you can't recognize the connection. So keep your eyes open, look at everything around you, and, most important, keep flipping your perspective around in other directions, even backward.

You just might find the answer.

Tony Baxter
Senior Vice President, Creative Development

When I started at Imagineering, I was assigned the design of a small but interesting merchandise shop. No sooner did I have that little shop looking great, than the project got canceled. I was devastated. Of course, I moved on to another project, and things were going great for almost a year—until that project was pulled as well. Was I a curse? I learned that I wasn't the only one this had happened to, and I sure wasn't going to be the last. Sometimes all our hard work goes by the wayside, but luckily we fill the void with something infinitely better, or at least something new to love. I've learned to move on and to let go.

April Sakai
Facility Designer
Architecture & Engineering

When we start a design, we write down a list of absolutely everything that we want it to do. Once the list is completed, what we thought we were going to build often turns out to be something completely different!

Principal Mechanical Engineer, Show Ride Engineering
Dave McCartney

Measure Twice, Cut Once!

Know That You Don't Know

It was a beautiful Southern California day. Sitting on my friend's patio, outside, under the shade of a large tree, sipping a cool Mexican beer … it was as though summer were eternal.

My friend offered me a slice of lime for my beer—a small, green-skinned citrus picked from that large tree. These limes tasted "peculiar," she said—perhaps they were some exotic type of lime. We thought nothing more about it until four months later when my friend rushed into my office to tell me that her lime tree had indeed been suffering an identity crisis. Those little green fruits were actually very young oranges!

This experience changed my friend's life. If we assume certain things to be true—that a tree is a lime tree, for instance—then every event that follows will be tainted by that assumption.

It's crucial to keep an open mind whenever something, for whatever reason, doesn't seem to fit. Listen to your gut. It's your best ally in approaching any challenge.

Bruce **Bruce Vaughn**

Executive Director, Research & Development

Imagineer Chris Carradine states that traditional problems are best solved through *analysis* followed by *action.* In contrast, complex problems are best solved through *action* followed by *analysis.* Traditional problems can be solved through modeling and optimization. However, complex problems are best solved through experiment and iteration.

When Imagineers are faced with a complex problem, they just start experimenting. We learn from our mistakes, so why not start learning as early as possible?

Ken Salter
Executive Director, Systems Engineering

One of the most gratifying aspects of my job is seeing our guests' smiles while enjoying an attraction that I worked on. This gratification is perhaps my strongest motivation toward putting in the long hours necessary to ensure success on a project. Finding a strong motivator will most likely lead to one's success in any discipline or career.

W. Joseph Carter
Senior Software Engineer, Scientific Systems

The most bang for the buck!

You Gotta Find a Way to Have It All

Like most industries, we are frequently faced with trade-offs in schedule, budget, and performance when we build a project.

But there is great resistance at Imagineering and at the parks to accept such trade-offs. There are usually powerful constituents on each side unwilling to give in. They constantly push the designers to find a way to have it all.

I soon realized that trade-offs come from the solutions we choose, not from the problems we're solving. So when faced with a trade-off, I know that we can often find a solution that avoids it altogether. There is often a way to reach the goal faster, cheaper and better. We just have to find it.

It's not uncommon for us to completely rethink our plans, reexamine our requirements, and go back to the drawing board in an attempt to have it all.

Jim

Jim Jaskol
Group Leader, Ride Control, Scientific Systems
Show/Ride Engineering

The Value of Ideas, Part III

Ideas and advocacy

It's not enough to throw ideas around in a brainstorm session. It's not enough to write them down in a meeting. It's not enough to flash drawings everywhere.

Sometimes it takes a while for ideas to percolate into people's minds *(especially other people's ideas into my mind)*. It's great to have all the drawings and reference, in an accessible room or a corridor or an adjacent space. It's more natural to take time to study the stuff and think or have an ad hoc conversation. Many times ideas come up, people react, and the ideas are gone.

While that helps ideas circulate, it's still not enough unless one idea naturally comes to dominate. An idea needs advocates to survive. Someone that trusts an instinct about it, looking at ways to keep it alive, or to revive it when it seems to be appropriate.

Sometimes a person at the top provides that, but it's also important that the momentum be sustained by other team members as well (or instead). That's where advocacy and instinct come in.

It's risky to fight for an idea, of course. It kind of goes against the image of the dispassionate and detached professional. What we do is art of a kind—we're in show business, like it or not. The guests pay to be entertained. Our product has to include caring and passion, not just formulaic cold procedure.

My note to self: "If an idea feels strong, stick to it and fight for it."

Ideas as layers

This is one of my pet notions. I firmly believe that a story, a place, an attraction at a theme park, a room or a graphic can never be about only *one* idea. I think those simplistic presentations just don't play well to audiences anymore. Today's sophisticated guests expect more.

It makes no sense to make a room all about a video presentation, about one prop (no matter how large), one character, etc. And yet for a lot of reasons we can wind up doing it—usually because of budget. That one principal idea has to be supported by secondary elements with their own reason for being. I have heard the concern that it can confuse the focus; it doesn't, if it's done right and if the idea is strong enough.

Layering the ideas does a lot of good things for a show, among them:

· It makes for a "generous" presentation, very important at a time where the most blatant crime is looking cheap—people are extremely value conscious.

It drives the story message home from different angles: as any teacher will point out, people take things in, in different ways.

It forces us to think of the show in a broader sense, and can make for great hints at ideas outside the show that would be too big to include.

It makes for less risk—a single idea is not the *single* bet to carry the whole show.

It allows for multiple viewing.

My note to self: "Even when we have the main notion, keep looking for complementary ideas to flesh it out. And later in the process, don't get talked or cornered into giving up everything for the single thing you have to get."

About everyone knowing where you are:

In my mind the dynamic process of making, exchanging, and building on ideas is truly fantastic. We get to see and to use some of the best of human abilities when we take part. Every bit that comes out is worth looking at carefully.

That pearl could slip by, lost in all the noise and the hustle.

I think it is natural for us hopeful types to think that there is always a better idea over the next hump. In fact, a lot of times the only clear conclusion to a problem is that the best solution is the one we are going to come up with next, the one we haven't invented yet.

Of course, we need to believe that, but just the same it's good to remember where your instincts took you first. Our guests' reactions to the experience will be instinctive and emotional—we need to tap into that, too.

Luc Mayrand
Senior Concept Designer, Creative Development

Ideas Take Time

You need to allow the time it takes to test an idea to see if it's worth pursuing. Gather a variety of ideas and test them all—let the bad ones fall away and the best ones surface.

Most important, allow the time and space to make mistakes. That's how we learn.

Mock up your ideas. Try them out first, to see if something is going to work. The mock-up doesn't need to be complicated—keep it as simple as possible. Often times, a mock-up reveals other solutions and sparks new ideas that would otherwise never have been thought of.

Don't get focused on what the idea will be when fully evolved—don't feel limited if you don't have the resources to accomplish the full end result right away. Concentrate on the resources you have and think about how you can continue to grow the idea to reach your ultimate dream for it. Do the best with what you have—then be prepared to nurture it and grow it to its full potential.

The Imagineers

As an engineer, I have many different "customers"—creative directors, manufacturers, architects, and attraction operators—each one pulling on me from a different direction. So now a difficult engineering problem seems impossible.

Instead of fighting these ideas, I've found it more valuable to remove my engineering hat and put on the creative director's hat to approach the problem from their perspective. This exercise gives me valuable insight, and sometimes that impossible engineering problem looks easy!

Chris Rose
Electronic Engineering

The relationship between an artistic mind and a technical mind can require some translation. The artist thinks in terms of forms and colors while the engineer thinks in numbers and physical relationships. The partners must find a way to bridge that communication gap so that the creative vision can be actualized—thus allowing both minds to participate fully in the final decision making.

Robert Bronsdon
Principal Engineer, Theatrical Design & Production

Smoke and Mirrors

Over the years, I have learned many lessons, but the one that I rely on most is knowing and growing the talent around me. Remember, no one knows everything, but everyone can learn. And as they say, experience is the best teacher.

My career in the Special Effects department started in 1979, working with a gentleman by the name of Yale Gracey. In my eyes, he was truly an original in the art of special effects. His designs baffled our guests some fifty years ago, and they still baffle guests today.

Yale and I shared an office at Imagineering, and we had a couple of days' downtime between projects. Yale instructed me to go out and design something. He didn't care what, he just wanted me to go out and design something.

I learned later that this was something Walt Disney often said to Yale—Walt would jokingly threaten to lock Yale into his workroom and not let him out until he invented something new!

So, in this same spirit I played around with our effects equipment, trying to get my design to work and starting to run into some obstacles. Yale came into our mock-up area periodically and saw the frustration building up in me of not being able to get past this one point in the design. He didn't say anything to me, just smiled and walked back to the office.

After a couple of trips and a couple of smiles, he finally looked at me and said, "Gary, I designed that same thing back in the fifties and ran into the same problems. This is what I did to fix it." Right there, I learned how valuable experience is—experience that comes from someone who knows what he is talking about, and experience that you gain by being allowed to explore, to learn, to fail.

Yale knew, as Walt knew, how to grow people's talents through letting them gain that experience. A person's stumblings today are their strengths tomorrow.

Gary

Gary Powell
Senior Principal Effects Designer, Imaging & Effects

If someone says, "You can't do that,"
our reply is, "Oh, yeah? Just watch!"

Chris Carradine
Vice President, Executive Concept Architect

I'm glad we didn't know
that what we
were doing was impossible!

Bob Gurr, Original Imagineer

At R&D, we're frequently asked to invent things that
have never been done before. We approach every
search with the attitude that what we seek exists
somewhere—we only have to find it. To believe the
impossible is the first step toward doing the impossible.

Ann Wheelock
Research Specialist, Information Resource Center

Sometimes the Answer Is Obvious, But the Solution Isn't

Imagineering is an entertainment company, not an engineering company. For engineers, this can be a little tricky. Engineers are taught to build things in the most efficient manner; form follows function, everything methodical, everything logical. And engineers speak in engineering jargon.

At Imagineering, it takes a large group with very diverse talents to create a Disney attraction, a list that goes on to include some 130 disciplines. Most of the people are not engineers. Using engineering jargon to explain a point to a project team usually gets a polite, blank stare. I have found that the most effective way to communicate is to observe how the discipline I am addressing communicates, and try to tailor my interaction in a way so it will understand my point.

In the early stages of designing the Grizzly River Run white-water raft attraction for Disney's California Adventure, the team was discussing how big the mountain should be that houses the ride. The show producer favored a very tall mountain, a big visual icon of the park. The project manager favored a smaller mountain, as rockwork and theming were very expensive. I wanted a just-the-right-size mountain so the water would flow properly, the laws of physics not caring one bit about the views of the show producer and project manager.

I could have pleaded my case by saying, *"In considering the coefficient of roughness, the trough hydraulic radius, the specific energy curve, and hydraulic and energy grade lines for a nonprismatic channel, I believe both supercritical and subcritical flow regimes will be compromised unless the mountain is the correct size."* Blank stares, for sure. Instead, I decided on a nontechnical, visual approach.

So I built a working flume model that could demonstrate the principles of open-channel water flow, and the pitfalls that can occur if the right height isn't considered. It was twelve feet long, made up of two-by-four lumber, a couple of plastic washtubs, and some plastic pipe. A little blue food coloring helped the water show up better, although I kept getting comments alluding to toilet bowl cleaners.

I advertised the demonstration as "Open Channel Water Flow for Non-engineers." I was able to show all the bad things that would happen without the proper height. The team even came away with an understanding of things like "hydraulic jump" and "supercritical flow," because they could see and touch them. In the end, I was able to convince the team that the just-the-right-size-mountain was what we really needed.

But there was still a bigger challenge we faced: the placement of the attraction within the Park. We engineers recommended placing the big water ride at the outer edge of the park. This lets us put all those noisy things like big pumps, ugly things like big pipes, and necessary things like huge water reservoirs "back of house," away from our guests and out of sight. Our creative planners had different ideas; they saw Grizzly Mountain as an icon, and wanted to weave it smack into the middle of the park. Not exactly our first choice!

The noisy pump issue was solved pretty easily by using pumps that were completely submerged under the water, and the ugly pipes were buried in the ground. But when it came to the huge reservoir, now that was a problem. Or what others who don't actually have to solve the problem like to refer to as an "opportunity."

The problem was space within the theme park— and the idea of using a fairly large amount of this precious commodity for a reservoir was quite unpopular.

We played with dozens of variations on where to put the reservoir, when suddenly someone looking at the map of the park—the same map we had all been looking at for many months—noted, "There's already a big lake in the park over by the boardwalk area—why can't we use that as our reservoir?"

The answer had been staring us right in the face, on a big map pinned to the wall. But the answer still wasn't the solution—there was one big remaining issue, a visual and thematic problem. When the ride starts up in the morning, water is pumped out of the reservoir up into the mountain until the ride is full, which makes the surface of the reservoir drop about two and a half feet ... and lakes don't do that (especially only parts of lakes).

In true Imagineering teamwork fashion, the creative team came up with its own elegant solution: the portion of the lake we needed to use as our reservoir would be themed as a tidal basin, where the level of the water naturally changes by several feet every day! Working together, we changed a liability into a wonderful showpiece.

It's easy to get caught up in the frenzy of over-the-top ideas, but don't overlook the plain, simple, it's-right-in-front-of-your-face idea. With the addition of a little teamwork and a few different perspectives, it may prove to be the elegant solution everyone is looking for.

Mark Sumner
Technical Director, Show/Ride Engineering

Sometimes You Have to Drown a Vice President

Problem solving is a necessary and valuable skill at Walt Disney Imagineering.

This is particularly true during the "Test and Adjust" phase of a project, where the complicated technology that makes up our shows and rides is brought together and operated for the first time.

In rare circumstances, the individual elements that make up an attraction operate as planned, and the system's test and adjust activities go smoothly. In most cases, subsystems have glitches and when these are sorted out, more fundamental problems are identified. It's like when you put wider tires on your car to make it handle better, only to find the new tires hit the fenders when you turn the wheels. *Ugh!*

One technique I use during test and adjust is called "everything—all the time." This means that when a problem is identified, you assign different teams to solve the problem in different ways and you work nonstop until the problem is resolved. If one approach fails, then you can fall back on one of the other attempts. If they all work, you can pick the best one. If none of them solve the problem, you just have to work a little harder to identify a new set of potential solutions and try again.

A good example of doing "everything—all the time" came during the test and adjust phase for Splash Mountain at Disneyland. We were struggling to solve a problem at a location in the attraction called the "dip-drop." The dip-drop occurs near the middle of the ride when the boat (which is themed to look like a hollowed-out log) transitions from floating in the water to rolling on a dry section of roller-coaster-type track, and is then reintroduced into the water where it floats for the rest of the ride. The track in this area is initially angled down so the log gains speed as it falls. Approximately halfway through, the track then rises back up to the starting elevation, which slows the log down to the normal speed. Everything was working as planned except that the logs were going way too fast at the end of the dip-drop.

This excess speed actually made the ride more fun—however, at the end of the dip-drop there was a hard right-hand turn where the speeding logs collided with the side wall. This resulted in a very rough ride, and if left as is, would have ultimately damaged the logs (not to mention the guests). It was time to implement "everything—all the time."

One team was assigned the task of "reprofiling" the hard right turn to smooth out the shape and allow the log to make the corner at the higher speed. This was a relatively simple task, since the waterway was much wider than the log, and we could install additional guide rails to increase the curve radius. Initial testing of some prototype guide rails was very encouraging.

Another team was charged with slowing down the boat by any means they could identify. They were making very little progress until someone had the bright idea to slow down the logs just like we slow down the Matterhorn bobsled cars at the end of that ride—by plunging the logs into a thin pool of water at the bottom of the drop. We had plenty of water, and an easy way to replenish the water after each log went through the pool.

Even though it was late in the day, we were so excited about this idea that we had to try it that evening. The dip-drop track is surrounded by a concrete pit with an open drain at the bottom to get rid of the unwanted water that drips off the logs. To build our thin pool, we simply plugged the drain and filled the pit with ride water. But how deep should the water be? We knew that we would have to find a compromise water level that would slow down empty logs as well as those filled with guests. In this initial testing, we would use only empty logs, just to see if the idea had any merit.

For the first trial of this concept, we filled the pit with enough water to put the low point of the track about two inches below the surface of the water. This way, the log would have to cut through a two-inch slice of water. We dispatched a test log and anxiously awaited the arrival of the vehicle at the dip-drop. The results were disappointing—the log flew through the water with no reduction in speed and hit the wall hard. Clearly, more water was needed.

We increased the water level to about eight inches. We wanted to make sure we saw some reduction in log velocity and increased the water level accordingly. We took our positions to view the test and called for the dispatch of one more log.

Unbeknownst to the Engineering team conducting the test, two of Imagineering's senior creative executives had arrived on-site just before this final test—and they both wanted a ride. Our team of ride operators respected their wishes and, unfortunately, loaded them in the test log before it was dispatched.

When the log engaged the eight-inch depth of water in the dip-drop, the results were dramatic. The log immediately decelerated and generated a wall of water that sprayed everywhere. A wave crested over the front of the log into the passenger compartment, thoroughly soaking the riders. The log tried to climb the track out of the dip, but because its speed had been reduced (and it was now carrying quite a bit of water) it didn't have the momentum to fully crest the following hill. So it rolled backward into the water pool, again throwing up another impressive wall of water and associated wave into the log—this time from the rear.

After a couple more cycles of the log going backward and forward through the pool—each time generating another impressive wall of water—the log finally stopped with two thoroughly soaked and very angry passengers. The Engineering team decided on the spot that the testing was finished and had showed no promise of success, and that we were done for the night. We hightailed it out of there before anyone could ask questions, and the next day permanently installed the prototype guide rails to smooth out the curve.

Splash Mountain successfully opened to the public a couple of months later and has become one of the most popular attractions at Disneyland.

Oh, and those creative executives did eventually dry out.

Don Hilsen

Technical Vice President, Show/Ride Engineering

Chuck Ballew

Concept Designer, Creative Development

When you're sitting in the bathtub, have you ever tried to grab a bar of soap? If you try to grab it too quickly, it pops out of your hand. But if you sneak up on it ... slide your hand under it slowly ... you'll be able to pick it up on the first try.

What Makes You Weak in the Knees?

What makes your heart skip a beat, what invigorates you, what ignites your passion, what gives you your edge, what keeps you in the game, and what makes you say it is good to be alive?

Ten years ago, as I began working on the landscaping designs for Disneyland Paris, I was standing in a French beet field, ankle deep in mud, when an epiphany came over me. It occurred to me that I was professionally at my best when I was able to sustain and nurture those same endorphins that made me "weak in the knees." For me to maintain that creative exuberance, I needed to develop a design philosophy that would keep both my outlook on design and my design ideas fresh, new, and challenging.

So, I came up with a series of guidelines: to better my last design, to take design risks, to take my design in a direction that is "uncomfortable" to me, to break away from the expected, to avoid the path of least resistance, and to try to push my designs beyond my reach.

To sustain your "weak in the knees" invigoration, you need to push your envelope. The question that kept me up nights was where should I look for design inspiration? What influences the creation of a well-planned and -executed design?

Since my early professional days, I have kept a file that is unnamed, unassuming, and filled with unusual and interesting clippings. Their only relationship to one another is that they captured my interest. They represent many design disciplines and mediums, yet fundamentally exhibit the same creative tools: shape, form, texture, scale, and color. They are my inspirations.

Painting is not always taking a brush to a canvas. Paint reduced to its common denominator is nothing more than a collection of colors. "Painting" for a landscape architect can be the choice of multicolored grasses or the arrangement of blooming flowers.

Allow yourself to see beyond what is in front of you, read between the lines, strive for personal greatness and betterment, challenge yourself, and push your envelope. Nurture and above all protect "what makes you weak in the knees."

Becky Bishop
Landscape Architect

I purposely look for crackpot and harebrained ideas to see if any of them shows potential. When I talk to a vendor about my application and he says, "Oh, yeah, you use the material like this," I usually lose interest. There is no use in trying an approach that everyone else knows about. But if a vendor tells me, "Oh, no, nobody does it that way ... " I get all excited since I know I've hit pay dirt.

Mark Huber
Technical Staff, Research and Development

Direct your passion. Achieve your result.
Always do your best and you will avoid regret.
Pass on your knowledge without reluctance.

John Mazzella
Show Producer, Creative Development

Never work on a project so large, its failure can't be hidden in a desk drawer.

It's easier and far more comfortable to stay in a rut, but unless you're on a ride at one of our theme parks, no one ever found true happiness following the same old track around and around.

Deadlines and the lack of deadlines—there are times when I need not worry about when something needs to be done, there are other times I have to have a deadline. I need to relax, I need to work like crazy, I need to be organized, I need to be disorganized. Sometimes I have a gut feel, I'm a bit uncomfortable because things are a little too organized. Sometimes you need some disorganization to force you to take a wrong turn and see where it leads!

Chris Runco

THE BEARVILLE TEDDY BEAR STORY

A FABLE WITH A LITTLE MESSAGE

by GEORGE SCRIBNER

Once upon a time, there was a little town called Bearville.

And this Christmas all the children decided (as children do) that all they wanted was a little teddy bear.

And soon Santa had his two teddy
bear manufacturers hard at work.
(I mean the elves can't do it all.)

One of the bear manufacturers
had a big meeting ...

... and the next day asked Santa
for more time and money.

Meanwhile, the other company
also set out to work ...

"Hmmm ... Now what are we trying
to do and how much time do we
have?" they all asked.

Then they promptly went to work,
making the bestest teddy bears
they could.

Well, the big day arrived.

And as the sun came up over Bearville ... "Waa! Waa!" What was that sound?

It was coming from the children who had gotten teddy bears made ...

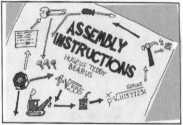

by "The Very Expensive and Late Company."

"Yea! Yea!" Yup, it was coming from the children who had gotten teddy bears made by "The Smart and Lean Company."

Just what they had asked for.

And for those of you who still aren't sure what my little story was all about—well, here it is ...

You see, it's not how expensive or fancy something is that makes it special ...

No, it's really much simpler. It's the idea that's important. Is it good? Is it fun? Do I get it? Simple, huh?

Oh, and in case you were wondering, Santa had a nice talk with the Boss at "The Very Expensive Company" and ...

... he's now selling car parts in Florida.

George Scribner

Creative Executive, Theme Park Productions

195

Adopting and Adapting the Imagineering Way

Listen to your dreams …
practice your skills …
grab the moment and make it yours.

For me the key to being an Imagineer is allowing the Child in me to have FULL reign. I refuse to let go of the Child that looks for FUN and allows me to approach

IMAGINEERING FROM A KID's Point of VIEW
Here's a few of my favorite "Kid tips".....

Look for the Grey

Kids are delighted to explore an endless range of possibilities. Everything has creative potential.

Look for Wonder

Kids notice things like butterflies, sand dollars, and soap bubbles and are able to see the wonder in each.
Do You?

Force Connections

Kids have a way of combining seemingly unrelated elements— thus creating new ideas. This helps the mind see relationships differently opening it up to fresh connections.

Change Hats!

Kids are great at pretending to be a fireman or princess. You gain new perspective by putting yourself in a different situation.

Allow Yourself
to DREAM
Kids spend a lot of time
imagining all sorts of strange
and wonderful things. This
opens your mind to a NEW
world of possibilities!

Break the RULES

Kids move boundaries, add players, or change the point system. This opens the mind to possible creative alternatives.

Play without Bounds or Judgments

As adults we are taught to be severe critics of anything impractical or flippant. Kids on the other hand routinely practice doing the impractical and flippant. Play without bounds allows the free flow of ideas without judgment.

Make it **Fun**!
My motto "If it ain't FUN-it ain't done" Kids know the value of humor and playfulness Great ideas flourish in an atmosphere of fun and silliness!

Joe Lanzisero
Creative Vice President, Creative Development

Top Ten Traits That Will Turn You From a Dreamer Into a Doer

1. Maintain a clear vision.

Always have a clear idea of where you are going—and take along a road map for others to follow.

2. Be optimistic—it's more fun!

You can be optimistic without being Pollyanna-ish. It's much more fun to be around optimists than pessimists.

3. Make curiosity your search engine.

It's amazing how many interesting things and people you can find and meet if you *never* stop searching and learning.

4. Be confident—believe in your ideas.

If you've done your homework and are ready to turn that project on, have *confidence* in your team and yourself.

5. Celebrate creativity.

You would be amazed at where creative ideas can come from, if you remember that no idea—no matter how "dumb" it may sound—is a "bad" idea. Don't put anything down; celebrate differences.

6. Use storytelling to involve your audience.

We communicate in many ways at Disney. We tell stories with trash cans and colors and costumes. And we communicate with visual literacy—eliminating things that *contradict* the idea, the theme, or the story.

7. Wear your guests' shoes.

At the Disney parks, we don't have "customers"—everyone is our guest. In this day and age of computer simulation and virtual reality, we are truly empowered with the tools to walk through the physical things we create, long before the first bulldozer arrives on a construction site. Wear your guests' virtual shoes first. Then, after you build it, use that simulation so you understand what you did wrong—and right!

8. Organize the flow of people and ideas.

My colleagues and I are constantly annoyed by the confusion caused by designers who do not "worry the details"—first and foremost about how their creations are actually used by the purchasers. In the early days, Walt Disney sent his designers to Disneyland to study where people wanted to go—and only then did he pave all the sidewalks and pathways.

9. Avoid overload—tell one story at a time.

Even before the word "download" found its place in our lexicon, the tendency to "dump" on even our friends—to make sure they know what we know—is often too tempting to resist. But the true act of communication is knowing when "enough's enough"! Avoid overload—tell one story at a time.

10. Take a chance.

Remember that quote from Walt Disney—"Now that I'm a grandfather and getting on in years, I hope I never forget that you have to keep marching in the parade. You have to be willing to *take a chance*."

Marty Sklar
Vice Chairman and Principal Creative Executive

John Horny
Concept Designer

One little spark of inspiration
Is at the heart of all creation
Right at the start of everything that's new
One little spark lights up for you

Imagination, Imagination
A dream can be a dream come true
With just that spark in me and you

"One Little Spark" by Richard M. Sherman and Robert B. Sherman